CHRISTIAN HIGH SCHOOL RELIGION SERIES

The Church Takes Shape

A Study of Church History

Student Book

By Robert C. Sauer

CPH
SAINT LOUIS

Write to Library for the Blind, 1333 S. Kirkwood Road, St. Louis, MO 63122-7295, to obtain *The Church Takes Shape* (Student Book) in braille or sightsaving print for the visually impaired.

The quotations from the Lutheran Confessions in this publication are from *The Book of Concord: The Confessions of the Evangelical Lutheran Church,* ed. by Theodore G. Tappert. Fortress Press © 1959. Used by permission of the publisher.

The quotations of E. G. Schwiebert in this publication are from *Luther and His Times: The Reformation from a New Perspective,* by E. G. Schwiebert. Copyright © 1950 by Concordia Publishing House.

Unless otherwise stated, the Scripture quotations in this publication are from The Holy Bible: NEW INTERNATIONAL VERSION, © 1973, 1978, 1984 by the International Bible Society. Used by permission of Zondervan Bible Publishers.

Copyright © 1988 Concordia Publishing House
3558 S. Jefferson Avenue, St. Louis, MO 63118-3968
Manufactured in the United States of America

All rights reserved. No part of this publication may be reproduced, stored in a retrieval system, or transmitted, in any form or by any means, electronic, mechanical, photocopying, recording, or otherwise, without the prior written permission of Concordia Publishing House.

2 3 4 5 6 7 8 9 10 11   06 05 04 03 02 01 00 99 98 97

Contents

To the Student   4

Unit 1: Power Plays in the Early Centuries   5
  1   The Gospel, the Power of God   6
  2   Augustine's *City of God* and its Consequences   8
  3   Islam and Iconoclasm   10
  4   Monasticism: Escape from or to Reality?   12
  5   The Papacy: The Peak of Power   14
  6   The Crusades: "God Wills It"?   16
  7   Schism, Seven Sacraments, and Scholasticism   18
  8   The Babylonian Captivity of the Church and the Early Reformers   20
  9   Reformation Eve: East and West   23
 10   Concluding Activities for Unit 1   25

Unit 2: The Reformation Era   26
 11   Luther's Early Life   27
 12   Luther: Monk and Priest   29
 13   Indulgences and Theses   31
 14   Luther the Writer   33
 15   Other Reformers   35
 16   Luther and His Family   37
 17   Zwingli and Calvin   39
 18   The Reformation Spreads   41
 19   The Formula of Concord   43
 20   Concluding Activities for Unit 2   45

Unit 3: Christianity after the Reformation   46
 21   Pietism   47
 22   Methodism, Rationalism, and Deism   49
 23   Christians Come to America   51
 24   Religious Revivals in Early America   53
 25   19th Century Mission Activities   55
 26   The Church and Social Issues   57
 27   19th Century Threats to Christianity   59
 28   Fundamentalists Battle Evolutionism   61
 29   Millennialism   63
 30   Concluding Activities for Unit 3   66

Unit 4: Christianity in the 20th Century   67
 31   Lutherans Come to America   68
 32   Growth of the Missouri Synod   70
 33   Kierkegaard, Barth, and Lewis   72
 34   Vatican II   74
 35   Historical Criticism   76
 36   Church Unions   78
 37   The Charismatic Movement   80
 38   The Television Evangelists   82
 39   The New Evangelicals   84
 40   Concluding Activities for Unit 4   86

Unit 5: The Lutheran Church—Missouri Synod Today   87
 41   Doctrinal Controversy in The Lutheran Church—Missouri Synod   88
 42   Mission Activities of The Lutheran Church—Missouri Synod   90
 43   Training Professional Church Workers in The Lutheran Church—Missouri Synod   92
 44   Social Ministry in The Lutheran Church—Missouri Synod   94
 45   Concluding Activities for Unit 5   96

To the Student

During Sundays in January, February, and March of 1987, George Vandeman hosted a TV series called "What I Like about
- the Lutherans";
- the Baptists";
- the Methodists";
- the Charismatics";
- the Catholics";
- Our Jewish Friends";
- the Adventists."

These are not all the church denominations in the world, but the group includes some of the major ones. Probably some of your friends and neighbors are members of these churches, and you may have had occasion to discuss religious matters with them. Maybe you have wondered when and why church bodies come into existence, what beliefs are important in each, and to what extent confessional Lutherans agree or disagree with them.

The sessions in this book will acquaint you with the origins of church bodies and where we Lutherans fit into the picture. May the Spirit of God through His Word bless your studies and give you a deep appreciation of the saints who contended for the faith (**Jude 3**).

UNIT 1
Power Plays in the Early Centuries

Our sinful nature manifests itself in many ways, and the desire to dominate one another is not the least of these. C. S. Lewis wrote, "I am very doubtful whether history shows us one example of a man who, having stepped outside traditional morality and attained power, has used that power benevolently" (*The Abolition of Man*, 1947).

The sessions in unit 1 focus on major power plays that plagued the church from the 4th to the 15th century, sometimes referred to as the medieval period, or the Middle Ages. Invading Germanic tribes brought about the collapse of the Western Roman Empire at the close of the 5th century. The 7th century witnessed the rapid spread of Islam in the East.

Within the church another power emerged, the papacy, which would reach its zenith under Innocent III (pope 1198–1216), who claimed to be the vicar of Christ on earth, superior to everyone.

In spite of these power plays, missionary efforts throughout Europe resulted in conversions. The truly great power—the Gospel—brought many to a saving knowledge of Jesus Christ, demonstrating the Biblical truth that **"in all things God works for the good of those who love Him, who have been called according to His purpose" (Romans 8:28).**

SESSION 1

The Gospel, the Power of God

"NOT SO WITH YOU" "YOU WILL BE BLESSED"

Our Lord warned His disciples about the desire to lord it over one another:

"**Jesus called them together and said, 'You know that those who are regarded as rulers of the Gentiles lord it over them, and their high officials exercise authority over them. Not so with you. Instead, whoever wants to become great among you must be your servant, and whoever wants to be first must be slave of all. For even the Son of Man did not come to be served, but to serve, and to give His life as a ransom for many'** " (Mark 10:42—45).

On another occasion, when Jesus had finished washing His disciples' feet, "**He put on His clothes and returned to His place. 'Do you understand what I have done for you?' He asked them. 'You call me "Teacher" and "Lord," and rightly so, for that is what I am. Now that I, your Lord and Teacher, have washed your feet, you also should wash one another's feet. I have set you an example that you should do as I have done to you. I tell you the truth, no servant is greater than his master, nor is a messenger greater than the one who sent him. Now that you know these things, you will be blessed if you do them'** " (John 13:12—17).

Jesus knew that not only outright enemies of the cross would disturb and trouble His blood-bought church; so would men chosen to lead the flock of God. He recognized that sin and the devil are hard at work in the church. Some suggest that the devil works harder to bring down the church from within than from without. In particular, power threatened to destroy the oneness that Christians have with one another.

Ironically, the church—in all ages—has in its possession a power that is greater than that which the secular forces generate in order to rule and dominate. It is the power of the Gospel.

THE GOSPEL, GOD'S POWER

The apostle Paul begins the epistle to the Romans with this clear confession: "**I am not ashamed of the gospel, because it is the power of God for the salvation of everyone who believes: first for the Jew, then for the Gentile**" (Romans 1:16).

What, exactly, *is* the Gospel?

The Formula of Concord, the last of the documents comprising the confessions (beliefs and teachings) of the Lutheran Church, says it well:

The little word "Gospel" does not always have one and the same meaning but is used in a twofold way, both in the Holy Scripture of God and by ancient and modern theologians. In the one case the word is used in such a way that we understand by it the entire teaching of Christ, our Lord, which in his public ministry on earth and in the New Testament he ordered to be observed. Here the term includes both the exposition of the law and the proclamation of the mercy and grace of God, his heavenly Father, as it is written in Mark 1:1, "The beginning of the Gospel of Jesus Christ, the Son of God." Shortly thereafter the chief parts are announced, namely, repentance and forgiveness of sins (Mark 1:4) . . . .

Likewise, Paul calls his entire teaching the "Gospel" (Acts 20:24) and summarizes it under these heads: repentance to God and faith in Christ. And when the word "Gospel" is used in its broad sense and apart from the strict distinction of law and Gospel, it is correct to define the word as the proclamation of both repentance and the forgiveness of sins. For John, Christ, and the apostles began in their preaching with repentance and expounded and urged not only the gracious promise of the forgiveness of sins but also the divine law.

In addition, however, the word "Gospel" is also used in another (that is, in a strict) sense. Here it does not include the proclamation of repentance but solely the preaching of God's grace. . . .

The Gospel . . . is that doctrine which teaches what a man should believe in order to obtain the forgiveness of sins from God. . . . The content of the Gospel is this, that the Son of God, Christ our Lord, himself assumed and bore the curse of the law and expiated and paid for all our sins, that through him alone we re-enter the good graces of God, obtain forgiveness of sins through faith, and are freed from death and all the punishments of sin, and are saved eternally. . . .

Accordingly every penitent sinner must believe—that is, he must put his confidence solely on the Lord Jesus Christ, "who was put to death for our trespasses and raised for our justification" (Romans 4:25), who "was made sin though he knew no sin, so that in him we might become the righteousness of God" (2 Corinthians 5:21), who was "made our righteousness" (1 Corinthians 1:30), and whose obedience is reckoned to us as righteousness in the strict judgment of God. Thus the law . . . is a "dispensation of condemnation" (2 Corinthians 3:6, 9), but the Gospel is "the power of God for salvation to everyone who has faith" (Romans 1:16)

Solid Declaration, V, 3–22

FOR DISCUSSION

1. Give examples of situations in which power plays an important role—in your own life, your school, your community, our country, or the world.
2. Think of a time when you were in power—when you controlled the power of the situation. Describe the situation. What did it feel like to be in power?
3. Think of a time when power was used against you—when you were controlled by a superior power. How did you feel?
4. Discuss power in your classroom. How should the teacher, who is in control, use power?
5. The well-known phrase "power tends to corrupt" seems to imply that power itself is evil. Is this true? If not, what do those words mean?
6. Is the saying "no person is so virtuous that he (she) can be given unlimited power" true or false? Why?
7. Define "Gospel" in your own words.
8. Why is the Gospel "the power of God"?
9. In the sessions to follow, the power issue will surface again and again. Why do you think the following statement by Romano Guardini is true: "The love of power is oppressive in every sphere, but in the religious most of all" (*The Church and the Catholic,* 1953)?

A WORD FROM THE WORD

You answer us with awesome deeds of righteousness, O God our Savior, the hope of all the ends of the earth and of the farthest seas, who formed the mountains by Your power, having armed Yourself with strength, who stilled the roaring of the seas, the roaring of their waves, and the turmoil of the nations.

Psalm 65:5-7

SESSION 2

Augustine's City of God and Its Consequences

Soon after Christianity became the dominant religion of the Roman Empire, invading tribes forced their way into Europe. This resulted in a number of barbaric kingdoms coming into existence. The Visigoths (Western Goths) settled in Spain and southern Gaul, and Christian captives shared the Gospel with them. They, in turn, brought the Gospel to the Ostrogoths (Eastern Goths) in Italy, the Vandals in North Africa, and the Lombards in north Italy. Clovis, king of the Franks (Germany) learned about Christianity from his queen, Clotilda, a Burgundian princess.

While most of this occurred immediately after the time of Augustine, the importance of his defense of Christianity cannot be overestimated. The hand of God was evident, and what to some was a tragedy (the end of the empire) in the long run proved to be a blessing.

THE CITY OF GOD

Augustine of Hippo (354–430) was one of the greatest teachers of Christianity since St. Paul. He wrote *The City of God,* a 22-book work, in response to the most serious challenge the church encountered.

Augustine's father was pagan, and his mother Christian. Not until he passed the age of 30 did Augustine become a convert to Christianity. He was baptized in 387 and became a priest in 391 and, in 396, bishop of Hippo.

During this time Alaric, leader of the Visigoths, besieged and sacked Rome (408–410), the first time that the heart of the empire had been overrun in 800 years. Rumors spread thoughout the Roman world that Christians were to blame, suggesting that they had drained the strength of Rome. Marcellinus, a Roman official in North Africa, asked Augustine to refute the charge. As a result, at the age of 59, he started the first book of *The City of God.* He completed the 22d book (we might call them "chapters" today) in 426 at the age of 72.

The first 10 books answer the charge against the Christians. Augustine shows that Rome's greatness was not because of the former religion of pagan polytheism (many gods). In book 10 he contrasts Christianity with paganism. In the remaining books he interprets human society. The real enemies, he says, are not Rome and opposing forces. Rather, they are two very different "cities": the earthly, or secular (founded on conquest and sustained by violence), and the City of God (the visible organized church). He maintains that the earthly city should not exist unless it is ruled by the City of God.

The City of God made a sharp distinction between the sacred and secular, which even today has influence on our civilization. *Also, it laid a foundation for the theory of the papacy: the visible church empire ruled by the bishop of Rome.*

CHURCH ORGANIZATION

Even before Constantine became emperor (306) the priests, and particularly the bishops, were given more and more power and influence. The clergy became economically independent. Legacies and donations added to the wealth of the church. The bishop received a fourth of the property, the priests in his diocese a fourth, the congregations a fourth, and a fourth went to charity. Legal disputes not involving criminal cases were settled by the church. The clergy could even obstruct justice in civil courts. As the concept of ordination was developed in the church, the priesthood claimed special powers that derived from the "indelible character" (once a priest, always a priest) received at ordination.

PAPAL POWER

The notion of a chief bishop over all the church did not have the approval of the infant church, but gradual development of this concept predates even *The City of God.*

The Council of Nicaea (325) recognized the office of the *metropolitan.* Persons holding this office were to approve or reject ordination of bishops and to preside at church gatherings (synods). But the council also indicated that the bishops of Rome, Alexandria, and Antioch were superior metropolitans, or *patriarchs*. Later councils added the title to the bishops of Constantinople (381) and Jerusalem (451).

After the end of the Western empire in 476, the emperor at Constantinople assumed the sole rulership of what remained (in the east). This added prestige to the patriarch of that city. The bishop of Rome, however, challenged this, invoking the tradition that the apostle Peter had been the first bishop of Rome.

Even so, the patriarch of Constantinople was selected as chief bishop of the whole church at the Council of Chalcedon (451). But the struggle between the two did not end. In fact, the Great Schism, in 1054, would ultimately result from the conflict.

DOCTRINAL ABERRATIONS

Church (canon) laws and traditions began during this period. The church developed certain teachings and practices that could not be supported by Scripture, but only by tradition.

Many of these changes in the doctrine and life of the church may have been caused by unconverted pagans who *professed* Christianity, but transferred their heathen beliefs in gods to the veneration of angels, saints, images, and relics. Having come out of polytheism and emperor worship, pagan hero worship infiltrated Christian worship. Saints were believed to share God's power. Christians began to call on martyrs for intercession and to worship relics. These relics (for example, bones or clothing of martyrs; splinters of the cross) were thought to have miraculous powers, all the way from caring for the sick to raising the dead.

The adoration of Mary, the mother of our Lord, came into being later than the veneration of saints. The belief that Mary remained a virgin after the birth of Christ dates back to the 4th century. Ambrose (339–97), bishop of Milan, spoke of her as being a second Eve who cooperated with Christ in His atonement.

Historians indicate that the worship of Mary came from the Mediterranean area pagan beliefs in the Great Mother. Similarly, the pagan worship of images also took root among the faithful: pictures and statues of Christ, Mary, and the saints were placed not only in churches but in the homes, where candles were lit before them, and bowing and the burning of incense became the practice.

The Augsburg Confession (XXI, 1–4) points to Jesus Christ—not to saints or Mary—as the only Mediator. See also **1 Timothy 2:5; Romans 8:34;** and **1 John 2:1.**

SACRIFICE OF THE MASS

Several ceremonies were added to the rite of Baptism, but perhaps the greatest departure from Scriptural meaning had to do with the Lord's Supper, which came to be understood as a sacrifice (act of worship toward God) rather than a sacrament (God bestowing a gift on worshipers). The Supper ultimately became an unbloody repetition of the atoning sacrifice of Christ by the priesthood for the salvation of the living and the dead. The church taught that the consecrated bread and wine were changed into the body and blood of Christ (transubstantiation). Many altars were erected in the same church building where priests would offer masses for the living and the dead. The sacrament became a meritorious deed on the part of the worshipers.

The Augsburg Confession called it an "abominable error" to have taught "that our Lord Christ had by His death made satisfaction only for original sin, and had instituted the Mass [the Lord's Supper] as a sacrifice for other sins.... Manifestly contrary to [St. Paul's] teaching is the misuse of the Mass by those who think that grace is obtained through the performance of this work" (XXIV, 21, 28–29).

FOR DISCUSSION

1. Why did Augustine write *The City of God?* What were positive and negative results of that work?
2. In what ways are clergy today regarded as superior to the laity? In what ways are they not regarded as superior?
3. How do Christians today honor Mary? How do differences here affect our relationships with other Christians?
4. How does the sacrifice of the Mass differ from the Biblical doctrine of the Lord's Supper?

A WORD FROM THE WORD

Great is the Lord and most worthy of praise; He is to be feared above all gods. For all the gods of the nations are idols, but the Lord made the heavens. Splendor and majesty are before Him; strength and glory are in His sanctuary.

Psalm 96:4–6

SESSION 3

Islam and Iconoclasm

Five times every day one-fourth of the world's population turns toward Mecca, the birthplace of Muhammad, the founder of Islam. Also, millions of Muslims travel there every year. In this way they fulfill their obligation to make at least one pilgrimage to Mecca.

In this section we will touch on their beliefs, the life of Muhammad, and how Islam affected the church. But the struggle was not confined to battling powers outside of Christendom. There was strife within: the iconoclastic controversy.

MISCONCEPTIONS

News stories about "Muslim militants" or "Muslim insurgents" may give us the impression that all Muslims (people of the Islamic faith) are troublemaking fanatics out to destroy civilization. But most of the 800 million adherents are not fanatics or leftists.

In Islam, as in Christianity, the faithful do not always act the way their religion prescribes. For example, the Ayatollah Khomeini and Anwar Sadat, both Muslims, condemned each other's policies.

Another misconception identifies Islam with oil-wealthy Arabs. The vast majority are neither wealthy nor Arabs. The three largest Muslim nations are Indonesia, Pakistan, and Bangladesh.

Since Islam began around 600, it has had a reputation for fanaticism and violence, yet in some instances we see just the opposite. The Muslim conquest of Egypt in the 7th century was a model of kindness compared to the Spanish Catholic conquests of Peru and Mexico.

BELIEFS

A Muslim believes that there is no god but Allah (an Arabic word) and that Muhammad is his messenger. Allah revealed his will and commands to Muhammad in the 7th century; they are recorded in the *Koran*, the Holy Book of Allah. One gains entrance into paradise by "submission to God" (the meaning of *Islam*).

Muslims hold that the all-knowing and all-powerful Allah will judge us all according to our deeds on the Last Day. Allah is fair, but also merciful; the sinner who repents before Judgment Day will enter paradise, but the unworthy will endure a torment of fire. The person who accepts Allah as God—accepts the message he sent through Muhammad, prays to Allah, is honest and truthful, practices charity, lives modestly, avoids arrogance and slander, and defends the faith against unbelievers—will be admitted to paradise, a place of rich sensual pleasures.

The most important good work is to war against unbelievers, even to death. A drop of blood shed in a sacred war is of more value than two months of fasting and prayer.

The following constitute the "pillars of Islam":

1. **Faith.** Muslims often repeat the simple creed: "I bear witness that there is no God but Allah and that Muhammad is the prophet of Allah." Muhammad taught that Allah is the God of Abraham and Moses, and the Koran identifies Allah with the God of the Hebrews. Allah created all things including angels and "jinn" (mysterious creatures more prone to evil than humanity, from which the devil is said to have sprung).

Muslims reject the Christian concept of the Son of God as being one with God; Jesus is a prophet, but no more. While Allah from time to time revealed himself to others, the last of the prophets was Muhammad. Throughout the Koran the chief motivation for accepting God and his will is fear of Judgment Day and everlasting damnation.

2. **Prayer.** The faithful are obligated to pray five times a day: at dawn, noon, afternoon, evening, and at night. Group prayers are of greater value than private devotions. The place for prayer should be clean, hence the "prayer rug."

The summons to prayer is by voice, not by trumpet (as the Jews used) or wooden clapper (used instead of a bell by early Christians). The crier faces each of the four directions in turn, repeats the simple creed, and concludes with "Come to prayer. Come to salvation. Allah is great! There is no God but Allah!"

The sacred day of public prayer is Friday. Rich and poor gather together and kneel in the mosque. A sermon follows the Friday noon service; all men and boys are required to hear it. Muhammad did not forbid women to enter the mosque, but advised them that it would be better if they prayed at home.

3. **Ramadan: the month of fasting.** Muslims fast every day of Ramadan, the ninth month of their year.

Because they use a lunar calendar, the months rotate among the seasons. When the days of Ramadan are short and cool it's no great hardship, for the meal at dawn is sumptuous, and the break at sunset is enjoyable after the long wait. During Ramadan each Muslim should recite or hear the entire Koran. The observance of Ramadan, it is held, quiets the spirit, subdues the passions, gives a sense of unity to Muslims everywhere, and even atones for all of the sins of the year.

4. **Almsgiving.** The Koran stresses the obligation to share one's possessions. Widows, travelers, orphans, and the poor receive the shared blessings of those who have an abundance. No precise amounts are prescribed.

5. **The pilgrimage (the hajj).** As noted above, every Muslim must make at least one pilgrimage to Mecca. The Kaaba, the main shrine of Islam, is the central place of devotion. Inside the Kaaba is the Black Stone that "fell from paradise," a stone about eight inches in diameter mounted in a silver frame. It is believed to be the only remnant of the house of prayer built by Abraham, and Muslims traditionally kiss it. A number of other rituals are also followed during the pilgrimage.

A part of the pilgrimage requires the hearing of the story of Abraham: his obedience to God's order that Ishmael (not Isaac!) be sacrificed; how God kept Ishmael alive; and Hagar's departure from the Hebrews. Up to 1945 less that 38,000 persons made the annual pilgrimage; today the number is close to 1½ million, evidence of the growth of Islam.

MUHAMMAD

Muhammad (ca.570–632) was born in Mecca and raised by relatives without any education. He was a shepherd, then a merchant, and later a camel driver. The religion of his people was heathen. When he was 40 years old he appeared as a prophet, proclaiming the religion of Islam. His kinsmen did not accept his teachings, so he went to Medina where he was received with enthusiasm and where he established a theocracy.

From 633 to 732 his followers, starting in Arabia, conquered Syria, Palestine, Egypt, and Persia; two attempts to take Constantinople failed. They conquered North Africa in 707 and Spain in 711. In the Battle of Tours (732) Charles Martel finally stopped this conquest.

Islam, however, paralyzed the church in the East. The patriarchal seats at Alexandria, Antioch, and Jerusalem remained for some time, but the church did not progress or expand.

ICONOCLASM

A controversy over the use of images occurred in the Eastern church during the 8th and 9th centuries. Many believe that the Great Schism of 1054 (between East and West) may not have transpired if this disagreement had not taken place.

Pictures and images intended to teach converts were in abundance. Kissing them, bowing before them, mixing scraped-off paint with the elements in the Lord's Supper, and even worshiping them brought the criticism of Jews and Muslims. In 723 Caliph Yazid II ordered that all pictures be removed from churches in his kingdom. Some years later Emperor Leo III (the Isaurian) did the same. But Germanus I (patriarch of Constantinople 715–30) refused to obey the order, so the emperor removed him from office. Monks supported John of Damascus, who taught that as God is present in the Lord's Supper, so He is present in the image.

A determined emperor emptied the Eastern churches of images and directed the Western churches to do likewise. Pope Gregory II took issue with him, and in 731 Gregory III (pope 731–41) excommunicated the emperor and all iconoclasts (from the Greek *eikōn*—image; and *klaō*—break). But when the second Council of Nicaea (in 787) approved image worship, the argument became even more heated. In 814 Emperor Leo V (the Armenian) ordered that image worship cease. Finally, a synod at Constantinople reached a compromise in the early 840s that restored paintings and mosaics in the Eastern churches.

FOR DISCUSSION

1. Prior to this session, what attitudes and beliefs did you have about Muslims? Have they changed? If so, how?
2. Compare Muslim and Christian beliefs.
3. Islam states that Allah will judge you on how you lived your life. What do most Christians believe? What did Jesus say about this?
4. What motivates people to believe in God (or Allah, or other gods) in all non-Christian religions? What motivates Christians to believe in and obey God?
5. Why do you think so many people without religious convictions are attracted to Islam?
6. Imagine yourself as a reporter back in the 8th century covering "Icon Gate." Consider both sides. Present the Western and Eastern sides. Now editorialize. Whose side will you support? Why?

A WORD FROM THE WORD

The Lord knows the thoughts of man; He knows that they are futile. Blessed is the man You discipline, O Lord, the man You teach from Your law.
Psalm 94:11–12

SESSION 4

Monasticism: Escape from or to Reality?

Problems were occurring in the church—power plays within and outside forces trying to crush her. These problems disturbed those who wanted peace and time to meditate and pray. They willingly surrendered pleasures, comforts, possessions, and even the company of others in order to live a holy life. This important movement in the church was called monasticism (from the Greek *monos,* which means "alone" or "solitary").

EARLY EXAMPLES

Already before the Christian era, heathen religions had forms of monasticism. Hindu sacred writings are replete with stories of "holy hermits." Vardhamana (known as Mahavira, i.e., Great Hero; ca. 599–527 B.C.), founder of Jainism (a religion of India), was a hermit monk. The more widely known Siddhartha Gautama (ca. 563–483 B.C.), founder of Buddhism, left his wife and child at 29 and renounced his inheritance to live the solitary life. When he was 35 he claimed he received a great revelation: the highest good is to enter Nirvana, a state of absolute nothingness. Judaism also had examples of ascetics (who practice self-denial): Elijah, Elisha, John the Baptizer. Other examples could be found in pagan Greece and Rome.

HERMITS

The desert seemed an ideal place to get away from the wicked world and its distractions. Egypt is regarded as the birthplace of monasticism. Anthony (ca. 251–356), the first hermit of note, felt the call to the desert after he heard the story of Jesus and the Rich Young Man **(Matthew 19).** He was so moved by it that he sold his property and gave the proceeds to the poor. In the desert he gave himself to a life of poverty. He became famous enough to have imitators, some living alone and others in groups. They tortured themselves by wearing hair shirts, carrying heavy weights on their shoulders, and sleeping in thornbushes. Many refused to wash themselves. Dirt was thought to be close to godliness while cleanliness was an indication of sin. The biographer of St. Abraham, a hermit who did not wash his face for 50 years, wrote, "The purity of his soul was reflected in his face."

While the desires to avoid worldly evil and to get close to God were noble, the hermits misunderstood Christ's teaching and erred completely with the notion that "matter" was the seat of all evil.

MONASTERIES

Pachomius (ca. 290–346) is said to have organized the first Christian monastery in Tabennisi on the Nile (ca. 320). The monks prayed together no less than 36 times a day and did manual labor. Once a day they shared a meal together, in silence. Individuals wore hoods so they could not be recognized. A convent for women was set up nearby. By the time of Pachomius' death, 10 monasteries had been established in Egypt, and by the end of the 4th century almost every province in the Roman Empire had monasteries.

CHARACTERISTICS

The early monks practiced poverty, chastity, and obedience. They believed that this was the teaching of Christ and the apostles **(Matthew 5:3; 6:24; 16:24; 19:12, 21; 1 Corinthians 7:7).** Each monastery had its own rules, some more severe than others. Fasting especially was held in high regard; some monks would refuse food for as much as five consecutive days. The custom of eating only once between Monday and Saturday was common. In east Syria, Palestine, and Asia Minor, extreme kinds of mortificaton were practiced: each of the Stylites actually lived in a basket perched on a high pillar, and the Dendrites spent their days and nights on the branch of a tree. Still others ate only grass for food.

WORK

The Messalians (or Euchites) held that the life of a monk should consist solely of prayer; all work and other activities were condemned. This, however, was exceptional, for the vice of idleness was to be dreaded. Two kinds of work were prescribed: manual and intellectual. The early monks weaved mats or cultivated the soil. Proceeds were used to sustain the community itself or given to the poor and to prisoners. Other monks worked as bakers or carpenters or were involved in the fine arts.

The intellectual work was the reading, studying, and copying the Sacred Scriptures and other religious writings. Calligraphy, drawing, painting, and the illumination of manuscripts produced precious works of art. The actual workday usually consisted of 6–7 hours.

PRAYER, SILENCE, AND SOLITUDE

Following was a Benedictine monk's day from the 8th to the 10th century:

	WINTER		SUMMER
Rise	2:00–2:15 a.m.	Rise	1:45–2:00 a.m.
Matins	2:25–4:00	Matins	2:15–3:15
Prayers	4:00–5:30	Lauds	3:30–4:00
Lauds	5:30–6:00	Prime	4:30–5:00
Interval		Work	5:00–8:30
Prime	6:30–7:00	Tierce	8:30–8:45
Reading	7:30–9:30	Reading	9:00–11:30
Tierce-Sext	9:30	Repast	12:00
Work	9:45–2:30 p.m.	Siesta	
None	2:30	None	2:30 p.m.
Repast	3:00	Work	3:00–5:15
Vespers	4:00	Vespers	5:15
Reading and Compline	6:00	Repast	6:00
Retire	6:30	Reading and Compline	6:30
		Retire	7:00

The need for silence and solitude gave monastic architecture its principal characteristics. The monastery was enclosed by walls with only one gate to the "outside world." Communication with that world was subject to strict control. Certain orders emphasized silence and solitude while others made fewer rules concerning talking and being alone. At one time 37,000 monasteries existed in the West alone.

RULE OF ST. BENEDICT

Benedict of Nursia (ca. 480–550) was one of the greatest organizers of Western monasticism. He wrote a "Holy Rule," which is divided into 73 chapters that deal with all aspects of the monastic life. The abbot is the head of the monastery, assisted by his provost, or prior; the dean is at the head of every 10 monks. Each monastery should have a garden, a mill, and workshops. The monks are to care for guests with honor.

The rule was adopted throughout Europe as far north as England. Benedictines became the most expert craftsmen and farmers in the Middle Ages. They also did mission work in the Scandinavian countries.

NEW MONASTIC ORDERS

A number of new orders came into being from the 11th to the 13th century. For 200 years the monastery at Cluny took the lead in the West, placing itself under papal protection so neither secular rulers nor bishops had jurisdiction over it. The popes, supported by the monasteries, exempted them from paying tithes and from excommunication.

The Dominicans (black friars) and the Franciscans (brown friars) were mendicant (begging) orders who gave their possessions to the poor, preached repentance and love, and traveled from place to place, living on what was given to them. They were directly under papal authority, teaching in schools of higher learning, restoring the sermon to the Mass, and guarding the faith.

The Jesuit order emerged later during the Reformation.

FOR DISCUSSION

1. Discuss your notions, attitudes, and beliefs about monasteries.
2. Why do you think there once were so many monasteries?
3. Compare a monastery to a university.
4. Why did the hermits torture their bodies with weights, hair shirts, and thorns?
5. Look up the Scripture passages that were used to support poverty, chastity, and obedience. What message was Christ giving? How can we practice that message today?
6. How was monasticism a blessing for the church?
7. Make a schedule of a typical school day. Compare it with a day in a monastery.

A WORD FROM THE WORD

Seven times a day I praise You for Your righteous laws. Great peace have they who love Your law, and nothing can make them stumble. I wait for Your salvation, O Lord, and I follow Your commands.
Psalm 119:164–166

SESSION 5
The Papacy: The Peak of Power

Don't let anyone deceive you in any way, for that day will not come until the rebellion occurs and the man of lawlessness is revealed, the man doomed to destruction. He will oppose and will exalt himself over everything that is called God or is worshiped, so that he sets himself up in God's temple, proclaiming himself to be God.

Don't you remember that when I was with you I used to tell you these things? And now you know what is holding him back, so that he may be revealed at the proper time. For the secret power of lawlessness is already at work; but the one who now holds it back will continue to do so till he is taken out of the way. And then the lawless one will be revealed, whom the Lord Jesus will overthrow with the breath of His mouth and destroy by the splendor of His coming. The coming of the lawless one will be in accordance with the work of Satan displayed in all kinds of counterfeit miracles, signs and wonders, and in every sort of evil that deceives those who are perishing. They perish because they refused to love the truth and so be saved. For this reason God sends them a powerful delusion so that they will believe the lie and so that all will be condemned who have not believed the truth but have delighted in wickedness.

2 Thessalonians 2:3–12

The Lutheran reformers were convinced that these words written by St. Paul applied to the papacy. We will now concentrate on the rise, culmination, and decline of the papacy.

BEGINNINGS

According to a list compiled in the 3d century, Linus and Cletus were the successors to the apostle Peter, who was claimed to have been the first pope. Not until the 9th century did the title apply only to the bishop of Rome. "Pater" (father— derived from the Greek *pappas*) designated any elder or leading member of the church. While the bishops of Rome, as heads of the church in the capital of the empire, were respected and consulted, they did not regard themselves to be vicars of Christ, nor did they claim special authority.

In 313 the powerful Emperor Constantine assured the Christians of safety; in later years he even exhorted Roman citizens to become Christians. He did this to unify and stabilize the empire, not because he was converted to Christ. He gave Miltiades (or Melchiades; bishop of Rome ca. 310–14) the Lateran palace, a splendid mansion on ground formerly owned by the family of the Laterani, as his official residence. Soon after, Miltiades received a letter from the emperor asking the bishop to settle a religious dispute in North Africa. He was not successful; the controversy continued to rage for two centuries.

A month after the death of Miltiades, Constantine announced to the people of Rome, "We have chosen to approve Silvester as successor to Miltiades and to Peter the apostle, as representative of Jesus Christ." The assembly confirmed the selection. Silvester was the interpreter when Constantine and Miltiades met. Silvester accepted the alliance between the empire and the church, and none of his successors has ever deviated from this important step. The church has constantly been entangled with secular powers.

Five hundred years later the Donation of Constantine was forged when Roman churchmen were battling Eastern Christians over civil jurisdiction. The document revealed that the grateful emperor had given the Roman pontiff permanent rule over the lands of the West and the East. Not until 1,000 years passed would that writing be acknowledged to be fake.

The 14 popes following Silvester were either chosen by the Roman assembly and confirmed by the emperor or selected by the emperor and confirmed by the assembly.

Eventually another group, the cardinals, selected the pope. City priests of Rome were called cardinals (derived from the Latin *cardo*, which means "hinge" or "support") because they were the main supporters of the church.

Julius I (pope 337–352) decided that there were to be 28 cardinals. They became wealthy and powerful. Innocent IV (pope 1243–54) created the red hat (or cardinal's hat) as symbolic of the cardinal's office—the color red because the cardinals were to be ready to give their lives for the faith. Urban VIII (pope 1623–44) declared that they should be addressed as *eminentia* (Latin for *eminence*). After the 12th century their number was greatly increased.

Gregory the Great (pope 590–604) was indeed Rome's greatest pope; only three popes would have the epithet "great" after their names. He possessed the gifts of administration, diplomacy, and practicality. During his pontificate, sickness and famine plagued Rome. The Lombards and Eastern Romans posed a military threat, and there was unrest and dissension in the church.

Gregory gathered an army, paid its expenses, and made peace with the king of the Lombards. Under him the discipline, finances, rituals, and music of the church were all improved. He established the archbishopric of Canterbury, was a strong supporter of the monasteries, and was responsible for sending out a large number of missionaries. He won the struggle with the patriarch of Constantinople, who had assumed the title *universal bishop*.

THE PEAK

Under Innocent III (pope 1198–1216) the papacy reached the height of its power. He proclaimed himself to be the vicar of Christ, superior to all men, possessing two swords, the spiritual and the secular. He intervened in the war between England and France, forcing King John of England to hand all of England over to him and to pay him an annual stipend of 1,000 marks sterling.

He removed and seated kings; he kept the authority to determine the outcome of church and clergy court cases. Presiding over the Fourth Lateran Council in 1215, a year before his death, he led 2,280 churchmen and representatives of European princes to approve his dealings with secular rulers. The council confirmed the practice of taking the property of heretics. A subordinate place in society was given to Jews. The clergy were relieved of paying taxes.

DECLINE

A few days after the burial of Innocent III, the cardinals met in Perugia, Italy, to choose his successor. Because no progress was being made, the civil authorities locked the doors of the meeting place. Then they quickly elected the elderly Cardinal Savelli as Pope Honorius III; he died in 1227. His successor, Gregory IX (pope 1227–41), was also elected in haste. During his pontificate, heresy became an offense punishable by death. After 1252, torture was used to make the accused confess, and unrepentant heretics were burned at the stake. The Inquisition was fostered. Laws were adjusted so that one person could be accused of heresy for criticizing or opposing another.

Gregory IX succeeded in making the Holy Roman emperor, Frederick II, a mortal enemy. He declared Frederick to be the beast of the Book of Revelation.

When Gregory died he left in shambles the mighty empire that Innocent III had created. Chaos prevailed in and out of Rome, where not only the cardinals, but also households and families, were divided over his activities. Confusion marred worship, business, and government. The emperor invaded Italy, imprisoning two cardinals in the northern city of Capua, and marched to Tivoli, not far from Rome itself.

Orsini, governor of Rome, saw to it that the cardinals were locked in a large room and ordered them to pick a new pope. Living conditions in that "prison" were miserable, but not until the end of September (1242) did the cardinals get down to business. One faction favored a candidate of Frederick, but the other group wanted a pope acceptable to the French, Spanish, and Sicilians, who were proposing a war against Frederick. After almost two months, still in the same room, they elected Godfrey, bishop of Santa Sabina. Two weeks later he died, the only elected pope who had never been consecrated.

Not until the following June (1243) could the cardinals agree on a new pope. The years that followed were fraught with delays and indecisions.

FOR DISCUSSION

1. Were the Lutheran reformers correct in identifying the papacy with the "man of lawlessness" described in **2 Thessalonians 2**? Defend your answer.
2. In what way would worldly leaders such as emperors or dictators not fit the description in **2 Thessalonians 2**?
3. In what ways was Constantine's reign a blessing for the church? In what ways was it a curse?
4. Discuss the relations of church and state in Constantine's time and in our time.
5. Compare the pontificates of Gregory I (the Great) and Gregory IX.
6. What factors besides the poor leadership of Gregory IX contributed to the decline of the papacy?

A WORD FROM THE WORD

Therefore, you kings, be wise; be warned, you rulers of the earth. Serve the Lord with fear and rejoice with trembling. Kiss the Son, lest He be angry and you be destroyed in your way, for His wrath can flare up in a moment. Blessed are all who take refuge in Him.

Psalm 2:10–12

SESSION 6

The Crusades: "God Wills It"?

Already in the 9th century many church leaders regarded fighting to defend Christians to be a holy work. In 878 John VIII (pope 872–82) proclaimed absolution to Christians who died in the defense of other Christians when the Muslims invaded Italy. Alexander II (pope 1061–73) did the same in 1063 when Christians fought Muslims in Spain. This was not the same, however, as engaging in a war to convert "infidels" by force.

Among other things, the Crusades had a powerful effect on uniting various isolated segments of Christians from the 10th to the 12th century.

THE FIRST CRUSADE (1096–99)

Prompted by the Eastern emperor Alexius I, who wanted to regain Jerusalem and Asia Minor from the Turks, Urban II (pope 1088–99) made an eloquent speech at the Council of Clermont in November 1095. He urged Christians to stop their private wars, turn the strength of arms against the Turks, and retake the Holy Land. Since the fourth century, pilgrimages had been made to the land where Jesus was born, lived, died, and rose from the dead. In time the pilgrimages were looked upon as gaining merit before God. When the Muslim Arabs conquered Palestine in the 7th century, they tolerated the Christian pilgrims. But the Seljuk Turks, who came into power in the early 1070s, did not treat visitors kindly.

In his appeal, Urban recounted the suffering that Christians were undergoing in the Holy Land, how they were flogged, sold as slaves, and degraded in every way by the murderous Turks. He commended his listeners for their courage, discipline, and skill, and promised that participation in the crusade (derived from the Latin *crux*—cross) would gain absolution from sin. Urban assured them that if they would die in the effort they would enter heaven, and if they would not die they would experience the joy of seeing the sepulchre of the Lord.

The people responded, "God wills it!" Urban agreed. He then instructed the "soldiers of the cross" to wear the emblem of a red cross, signifying the binding nature of their intent (a vow that could not be rescinded), on their breasts or shoulders.

The people were so enthusiastic that they began the march before capable leaders were found.

Some mobs did reach Constantinople but they were massacred by the Turks in Asia Minor.

But 100,000 nobles and knights from western Europe met at Constantinople (1096) and laid siege to Antioch, taking the city (1098) after almost a year of battle.

Led by Godfrey of Bouillion, France, many of the crusaders went on to capture Jerusalem (1099).

THE SECOND CRUSADE (1147–49)

Again, eloquent speaking by one man, Bernard of Clairvaux, stirred up the people to march on the Turks, who had captured Edessa, Syria. The promise of a sure reward for those who put to death the unbeliever in the Holy Land was repeated. At the outset it appeared that this crusade would bring an end to the Turkish threats. However, the venture turned out to be a failure.

THE THIRD CRUSADE (1189–92)

Danger threatened again when Saladin, ruler of Muslim Egypt, began a crusade against the Christians, capturing Jerusalem in 1187. This gave rise to the third crusade. However, the people were motivated by romance, chivalry, plunder, and greed more than religion, although the usual spiritual rewards were offered by the pope. Success seemed assured, since the venture included Richard I (the Lion-Hearted) of England, Philip II (Philip Augustus) of France, Holy Roman Emperor Frederick I (Barbarossa), and their armies.

But Frederick died before he reached the Holy Land, and his army was disbanded. Philip and Richard quarreled, and Philip withdrew his troops and returned to France. By the time he reached Jerusalem, Richard realized that his army was too small to take the city, so he returned to Acre, a coastal city, where he scored a victory over Saladin. A truce was made and the Christians were given a long, narrow strip of territory by the sea and free access into Jerusalem, which was still controlled by the Muslims.

THE FOURTH CRUSADE (1202–04)

Innocent III was the prime mover in this effort. In order to regain the Holy Land for Christendom he tried to arouse the European rulers and the emperor to launch another crusade. When this failed, he appealed to the bishops and to all the faithful. The fourth crusade did not reach the Holy Land.

THE CHILDREN'S CRUSADE(S) (1212)

Stories of adventure led children throughout Europe to attempt a crusade of their own. Misguided preachers encouraged them, believing that they would be given supernatural power; did not our Lord Himself proclaim children to be the greatest in the kingdom? One boy, Nicholas, took a large group as far as the Alps, where the children died of starvation. Others were seized by Saracens and sold into slavery.

THE FIFTH AND SIXTH CRUSADES (1217–29)

The Fifth Crusade may be dated from 1217 to 1221, and the Sixth from 1228 to 1229. Appealing to the consciences of the faithful, Innocent shamed them for expecting boys and girls to shoulder their responsibility. While the army, headed by the patriarch of Jerusalem, made it to the Holy Land, Jerusalem remained in the hands of the Muslims.

CONSEQUENCES

The crusades failed to recover the Holy Land. Yet, some blessings resulted from the enormous loss of lives and money:

1. Christendom became united. Christians shared common ideas, and widespread good will was generated.
2. In a sense the grip of the papacy was weakened because it had promoted fruitless war.
3. Intellectual pursuits were stimulated. They led to study, travel, and new literature.

On the other hand, certain results were unfavorable:

1. Religious intolerance was generated by the crusades. This led to the Inquisition—a Roman Catholic search for heretics, followed by punishment or death.
2. A renewed interest in relics and shrines developed.
3. Money collected for the crusades formed the basis of a regular tax to be paid to the pope.

While foreign to the message of the Prince of Peace, the mentality of the Middle Ages agreed with the idea that armed force is acceptable for Christian armies if the cause is right. St. Paul does speak of fighting **"the good fight of the faith" (1 Timothy 6:12)**, of putting on **"the full armor of God,"** of taking **"the helmet of salvation and the sword of the Spirit,"** but these have to do with the Christian's struggle **"against the spiritual forces of evil in the heavenly realms" (Ephesians 6:12–17)**. He specifically states that **"though we live in the world, we do not wage war as the world does. The weapons we fight with are not the weapons of the world" (2 Corinthians 10:3–4)**. Paul exhorts Timothy "to endure hardships . . . like a good soldier of Christ Jesus" (2 Timothy 2:3–4), but the point here is that we should not become engrossed with civil affairs, lest the work of the ministry be neglected. Lacking any true Scriptural mandate, the crusaders were bound to fail.

"However," one may argue, "the crusaders halted the Moslem conquest of the world. Had Christendom not taken the initiative, it may have suffered great losses in East and West." But would Hitler have conquered the world if America had not intervened? We cannot reconstruct history or our own lives with "ifs."

FOR DISCUSSION

1. What was a crusade? What was its objective?
2. Discuss the various reasons why popes, kings, emperors, knights, soldiers, monks, priests, common men and women, and children took part in the crusades.
3. What actually were the outcomes of the crusades in terms of land conquered, money raised, integration of society, strength of the Catholic Church, armies trained, literature, art, etc.?
4. The crusades delayed the fall of Constantinople for over 300 years. Why was this a blessing for the Christian West?
5. It is altogether human to blame others for our misfortunes. Cite an example of this from the crusades.
6. Taking some of the consequences into account, were the crusades "the will of God"? Defend your answer.

A WORD FROM THE WORD

Many, O Lord my God, are the wonders You have done. The things You planned for us no one can recount to You; were I to speak and tell of them, they would be too many to declare.

Psalm 40:5

SESSION 7

Schism, Seven Sacraments and Scholasticism

SCHISM

In session 3 we noted that the iconoclastic controversy may have helped to cause a split in Christendom. One issue that was certainly a cause of the division was the addition of the Latin term *filioque* (FILL-e-O-kway) to the Nicene creed, namely, that the Holy Spirit proceeds not only from the Father but also from the Son. This was approved by Charlemagne (emperor of the West 800–814) in his *Libri Carolini* (Caroline Books).

Under Charlemagne a new Roman-Frankish empire was born. He promoted public education, maintaining that at least in the upper classes every son should be educated. He was very active in church government and organization. On Christmas Day 800 Leo III (pope 795–816) crowned him and identified him as emperor; this resulted in the relations between East and West becoming even more strained. While the East was willing to recognize the bishop of Rome as "first among equals" (first among the patriarchs), his alleged superiority became more and more pronounced.

Differences that may seem trivial paved the way for the inevitable break. These included the controversy over images, the addition of the words "and the Son" (*filioque*) to the Nicene Creed, and the magnification of the Roman bishop. Also, the East held that the invocation of the Holy Spirit on the bread and wine in the Lord's Supper brought about the change to Christ's body and blood, while the West insisted that the spoken words of institution were responsible for the change. At the same time, the West was developing doctrines of the immaculate conception of Mary, enforced clerical celibacy, and the use of unleavened bread in Communion. Further differences appeared among priests being shaven or unshaven and in different designs of vestments. Both East and West realized that something was not right.

Eventually Photius (patriarch of the East, at Constantinople) and Pope Nicolas I (of the West, at Rome) excommunicated each other in the 9th century (Photian schism). The matter came to a head in 1053 when Cerularius, then patriarch of Constantinople, sent a letter to the bishops of southern Italy in which he listed the errors of the Western Church. This angered Pope Leo IX, but Constantine IX (Monomachus; Eastern Roman emperor) tried to bring about peace by convincing the pope to send Cardinal Humbert and two other representatives to Constantinople and settle the issues. Peace was not to be. On July 16, 1054, the papal legates placed on the high altar of the church of Sophia a decree of excommunication. Cerularius and the other Eastern patriarchs responded by excommunicating Rome. The break—or schism—was complete.

Were there Scriptural reasons for the break? This important question applies to the issue of church fellowship, which continues today. In **1 Corinthians 1:10–17** Paul warns against divisions because of loyalties to certain leaders. In **Romans 16:17** he counsels Christians to **"watch out for those who cause divisions and put obstacles in your way that are contrary to the teaching you have learned. Keep away from them."** Lutherans hold that fellowship should be based on agreement on that which is clearly taught in Scripture. So the Formula of Concord (Solid Declaration, VII, 33) quotes Luther's words with approval: "Whoever, I say, will not believe this [the Real Presence in the Lord's Supper] will please let me alone and expect no fellowship from me. This is final."

SACRAMENTS

While *Baptism* and the *Lord's Supper* were regarded as the only sacraments in the early church, by 1215 the official number became seven. Added were Confirmation, Penance, Extreme Unction, Ordination, and Marriage.

Confirmation had already been regarded as a sacrament late in the 4th century. In the West, when children were 12, the bishop anointed their foreheads with oil and laid his hands on each one. It was believed that this action "confirmed" the grace received in Baptism. In the East, where the sacraments were called "mysteries," Baptism was administered by triple immersion. Immediately thereafter, the baptized were anointed with "chrism," a mixture of oil and other ointments consecrated by a bishop but applied by a priest on the brow, eyes, nostrils, mouth, and ears.

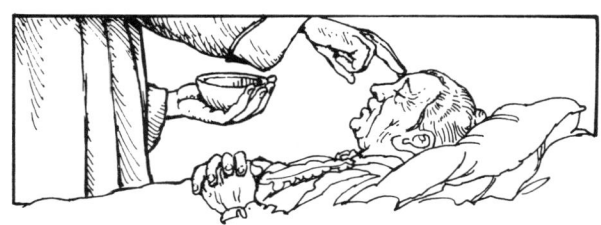

Penance began when the penitent, feeling true sorrow over sin and promising to improve, confessed his or her wrongs to the priest. The priest would then give absolution, or forgiveness, but certain works had to be performed as punishment, such as many prayers or fasting. The Fourth Lateran Council (1215) ruled that all baptized persons of the age of discretion must confess and do penance at least on Easter. The once-a-year rule was also mandated in the East, although the faithful were urged to "penitence" four times a year.

Extreme Unction, the anointing of the sick and dying with oil, was in use already during the pontificate of Innocent I (401–417). In the West it came to be reserved only for the dying, but in the East the purpose of the anointing and accompanying prayers was for the recovery of the sick. Unction had a full and an abbreviated form. The choice depended on the time available. The full form included the anointing of the eyes, nostrils, lips, hands, and feet (external sense organs). In the older rite, the loins were also anointed.

Ordination, also called *orders,* was limited to males. There were eight orders, four minor and four major. The former consisted of the doorkeeper, who admitted eligible persons to the altar and saw to it that the others left before the celebration of the Eucharist; the lector, who read the Scriptures (except the Gospel); the exorcist, who performed the rite of exorcism at baptisms; and the acolyte, who brought the bread, wine, and water to the priest at the altar.

The major orders were subdeacon and deacon, who assisted the priest during the celebration and helped in the distribution of the elements; the priest, whose chief function was to celebrate Mass and administer the other sacraments; and the bishop, the spiritual overseer of the community, who ordained priests and confirmed children. The East had similar orders.

Before the 12th century, marriage could take place among Christians without the presence of a priest. From the 3d century to this day, however, civil marriages—those performed by secular officials—were frowned on by the church. Charlemagne forbade marriage without the blessing of a priest. The East again emphasized the role of the Holy Spirit in this "mystery," regarding the invocation of the Spirit as essential to a Christian marriage.

SCHOLASTICISM

Earlier we noted that the crusades created a renewed interest in various kinds of intellectual pursuit and travel. It surfaced in *scholasticism* (the methods of thought generated by reason—"I do not reason to believe, but I try to reason what I believe").

Notable schoolmen included Peter Abelard, Thomas Aquinas, Duns Scotus, Roger Bacon, Peter Lombard, and William of Ockham. Two groups emerged: the *nominalists,* who thought that truth can only be obtained through reason, and the *realists,* who believed that human senses are not to be depended on, and that only revealed truth is reliable.

Scholasticism contributed to the rise of universities. They were established from Scotland to Spain and from Sweden to Italy.

By 1450 the printing press was used throughout Europe. Some 30,000 books were in print by 1500. However, the church at the time did not see the educational and mission value of the invention.

FOR DISCUSSION

1. Define *schism*. List general causes, dynamics, life history, and result of a schism.
2. Think of a "schism" in your life—with friends, relatives, neighbors, etc. Describe your experience.
3. List the reasons for the Great Schism of 1054.
4. Which of these reasons would we today regard as neither commanded nor condemned in Scripture?
5. Define *sacrament*. Why do we observe only two sacraments instead of the seven observed by the Roman Catholic Church?
6. How does our present Lutheran rite of confirmation differ from that of the Middle Ages?
7. What is the main difference between the Eastern and Western sacrament (mystery) of unction?
8. Define *scholasticism*.
9. Which statements coming out of scholasticism do you believe were valid?

A WORD FROM THE WORD

The Lord looks down from heaven on the sons of men to see if there are any who understand, any who seek God. All have turned aside, they have together become corrupt; there is no one who does good, not even one . . . Oh, that salvation for Israel would come out of Zion! When the Lord restores the fortunes of His people, let Jacob rejoice and Israel be glad!

Psalm 14:2–3, 7

SESSION 8

The Babylonian Captivity of the Church and the Early Reformers

THE BABYLONIAN CAPTIVITY

While popes continued to claim the powers that were in effect at the time of Innocent III, Boniface VIII (pope 1294–1303) was in trouble from the outset. Ignoring the spirit of independence and the feeling of nationalism that had been developing in the countries, he tried to be the mediator between Edward I of England and Philip the Fair of France.

Neither king listened to him. In 1296 Boniface issued an edict, or papal bull, that forbade the two from taxing the clergy and church properties. The kings, as one would expect, rejected this move. In retaliation, Boniface issued another bull, the famous *Unam Sanctam* (1302), in which he maintained that to disobey the pope was to disobey God, who had established the papacy. The bull declared that people had to obey the pope or forfeit their salvation. It was especially aimed at the French king, who had responded to the earlier bull by stopping money from leaving France and going to Rome.

Boniface then ordered the closing of churches and called a halt to marriages and to burial ceremonies in Philip's kingdom. The king sent his representative with troops of soldiers to Rome. They captured the pope and put him in prison. Boniface died a month later.

In 1309 Clement V (pope 1305–14), who was elected with the backing of Philip, moved the papal court to Avignon, France, where it would be headquartered for nearly 70 years. Immorality prevailed in the court, and church offices could be bought for money, which was used to pay for the luxuries. Historians called it the Babylon Captivity because a political power ruled the papacy like Israel was ruled by the Babylonians centuries before. The exile, or captivity, ended when Gregory XI (pope 1370–78) returned to Rome in 1377.

After Gregory's death, Urban VI (pope 1378–89) was consecrated. He declared that he would appoint a sufficient number of Italians to insure a majority in the college of cardinals. But the French cardinals objected and somehow convinced even the Italian cardinals that Urban's election was not valid. The entire college then elected Clement VII (antipope 1378–94). But Urban would not step down. For years the world lived with two popes, each claiming to be the true pope.

The dispute continued after the deaths of Urban and Clement. To seek a resolution to the problem, a council was called in 1409 at Pisa. They elected a new pope, Alexander V (antipope 1409–10), but popes representing the other two factions continued to stay in office. Finally, at the Council of Constance (1414–18), all three were deposed and Martin V (pope 1417–31) was chosen to be the one legitimate pope.

EARLY REFORMERS

Already in the days of Innocent III certain sects arose because of abuses in the church. The *Waldenses,* founded by Peter Waldo, arose about the same time. Though they were persecuted, the sect is still found in Italy. They elevated Scripture, denied the existence of purgatory, and gave laymen the right to preach and administer the sacraments. Poverty was held to be a most God-pleasing way of life.

William of Ockham (English scholastic philosopher; died about 1349) declared that in civil matters the state is over the church and the pope. He rejected papal infallibility and maintained that a council is a higher authority than the pope in the church. He believed that Holy Scripture is the only infallible source of doctrine and life. The councils of Pisa and Constance made efforts to take steps toward reform. The Council of Basel (1431–49) decided that the authority of a council exceeded that of a pope, but this was rejected by the pope himself. William also held that the true church was comprised of Christians who had been predestined to salvation and, since only God could know who they were, he upheld the concept of the *una sancta*—the one true church.

John Wycliffe (1320–84) of Oxford, England, generated a reform movement in England that echoed Ockham's teachings. But he went much further, stating that salvation is by faith in Jesus Christ, that the pope is the antichrist, and that in the Lord's Supper the bread and wine are not changed into Christ's body and blood.

Because Wycliffe's views were similar to those of Luther, he was later called the "Morning Star of the Reformation." Like Luther, he believed that the Bible in the language of the people was a "must," so he saw to it that the Latin Bible, the Vulgate, was translated into English, the first complete translation into that tongue, in the early 1380s. Gregory XI (pope 1370–78) condemned him, but the English Parliament protected him. By 1407, however, anyone who even possessed Wycliffe's books was put to death.

John Hus, (ca. 1370–1415) a lecturer at the University of Prague, Bohemia (now Czechoslovakia), a student of Wycliffe and a powerful preacher, denied the authority of the pope, rejected the doctrine of purgatory and saint worship, and like Wycliffe, held that Scripture was to rule in the church. After being excommunicated, he was taken to the Council of Constance, condemned as a heretic, and burned alive at the stake, though a large number of his followers tried to rescue him.

Girolamo Savonarola (1452–98) began his career in the study of medicine, but at the age of 23 he entered a monastery in Bologna, Italy. While his doctrinal views were not at variance with those of the church, he did advocate political and moral reform. He organized some 4,000 young people who confiscated and burned books and objects of art judged to be immoral. He called for Bible reading in place of attendance at theaters and participation in games. His opposition to the pope and his preaching against the corruption in the church ended in his being hanged and burned for heresy.

Meister Eckhart (ca. 1260–1327) was a mystic who wanted reform in the church but not by force. He felt this could be done by individuals seeking union with God. Constant thinking about God and being obedient to and content with His will were at the core of his teachings. Other prominent mystics were *Johann Tauler* (ca.1300–61), pupil of Eckhart, and *Thomas à Kempis,* (ca. 1380–1471), best known even today for *The Imitation of Christ.*

An extremist movement among the mystics led to organizations called Brothers and Sisters of the Free Spirit. Its advocates were convinced that people could die to themselves so completely that, being detached from their bodies, they could permit it to eat, drink, have sex, and carry out any such physical activity it wished. Was this not, they said, the teaching of Christ **(Matthew 10:39)** and the apostle **(Romans 6)**?

Thus, mysticism stressed communion with God, rather than salvation through Jesus Christ. It did, however, concentrate on true devotion—a reaction against the formalism that had become virtually the religion of many. In this sense it helped to open the way to the Reformation.

Gerhard Groot (1340–84) founded the *Brethren of the Common Life* in Holland, a group of lay people who also tried to reform the church but not break with its organization. They stressed education of the young and service to the poor. Thomas à Kempis belonged to the Brethren.

CHANGE

Change was bound to come. Patriotism, the revival of intellectual pursuit, an expanding civilized world, the use of the printing press, the discoveries of Galileo, the travels of Marco Polo, the discovery of America, Vasco da Gama's sea voyages, and Magellan's trip around the world belonged to this period (which continued through Luther's lifetime).

Even so, common people lived in a world of fear and danger. In answer to this, it was taught that security could only come from the church and her clergy, with sacraments that would accompany humanity from birth to death and even beyond. Purgatory was far more real in the system of belief than it is today, and because temporal punishments were exacted there, masses for the dead, prayers, relics, and pilgrimages were needed. The sale of indulgences was based on the notion that Christ and the saints did good works beyond God's demands and that these good works could be bought from the church to atone for the sins of the living and the dead.

FOR DISCUSSION

1. What was the main cause of the breakdown of papal power when Boniface VIII was pope?
2. Why was the period after Boniface VIII called the Babylonian Captivity of the church?
3. What effect did the simultaneous rule of three popes have on the church?
4. Name the early reformers and briefly describe their beliefs.
5. Besides forceful preaching and condemnation of the papal church, what other methods were attempted to bring about reform?
6. How did the church answer the fears of the common people?
7. How did God continue to preserve His Word during this period?

A WORD FROM THE WORD

Those who trust in the Lord are like Mount Zion, which cannot be shaken but endures forever. .... Do good, O Lord, to those who are good, to those who are upright in heart. But those who turn to crooked ways the Lord will banish with the evildoers.

Psalm 125:1, 4, 5

SESSION 9

Reformation Eve: East and West

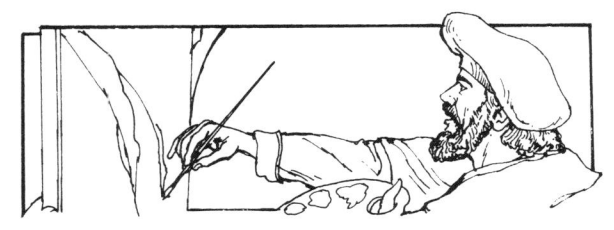

RENAISSANCE

The era called the Renaissance ("rebirth") began in Italy in the early 1300s, spread across Europe during the next 200 years, and ended about 1600—the time of Shakespeare.

The Renaissance was a cultural movement in which people tried to recapture the spirit of the Greek and Roman cultures in their own artistic, literary, and philosophic works. Among some people the movement emphasized this life rather than the next, worldly fame rather than eternal rewards, pleasures of the flesh instead of self-denial, success above justice, and free-thinking in place of being told what to think. Arts, letters, and the classics became popular.

Especially the upper class embraced the secularism of the movement: humanity is self-sufficient and has no need of God. We are the masters of our own fates and the captains of our souls.

The Renaissance urged its advocates to become proficient in as many skills as possible. For instance, we remember Leonardo da Vinci as a painter, but he was also an inventor, a mathematician, and an engineer. Michelangelo, who is best known for painting a series of frescoes that pictured the progress of the soul to God on the ceiling of the Sistine Chapel, was also a poet, a sculptor, and an architect. Well-rounded disciples of the Renaissance also showed concern for their physical lives. They would hunt, run, swim, dance, as well as immerse themselves in Latin and Greek.

During this time Alexander VI (pope 1492–1503) sired four illegitimate children, two of whom were the notorious Cesare Borgia and his equally vile sister, Lucrezia. Julius II (pope 1503–13) was so fascinated with war that he put on armor and personally led his troops over the wall of Bologna. Leo X (pope 1513–21), who occupied the papal chair at the time of Luther, was given to gambling and hunting. Tradition has it that he was the one who said, "The papacy is ours; let us enjoy it!"

While this was going on, a renewed interest in the forgotten legacy of ancient Rome swept through Italy. The elite collected Roman statues and classical pagan writings. Children were given long classical Latin names and learned to give orations in the classical Latin language. Astrology became popular, and even the popes sought counsel from its seers.

While some lived in open immorality and abandoned the true faith, others demonstrated excitement in connection with their faith in God. Not only in Florence, under the stern Savonarola, but throughout the land itinerant preachers held what today would be called "revivals" in town after town. Groups would meet together to sing hymns, but also to scourge one another ("flagellantism"—an act of public penance). Many believed in miracles, and the Franciscans attempted the truly great miracle of reconciling feuding families.

MEANWHILE, BACK EAST . . .

The Great Schism between East and West (1054) virtually ended all communication between the Eastern and Western churches. As heirs of the West, we may not have such a great interest in the East, but no study of church history would be complete without some mention of the so-called Greek (Orthodox) church. A thousand years after the birth of Christ, so the story goes, Prince Vladimir (956–1015) of Kiev, Russia, decided to investigate the existing religions with a mind to selecting the best. Neither the Muhammadan prohibition against the use of alcohol nor the fact that the Jews had to live away from their homeland impressed him. But when his representatives went to Constantinople to look at the Byzantine church, they returned with glowing reports about the magnificent buildings and liturgy. After this a good relationship developed between Moscow and Constantinople, so much so that when the Turks captured the Byzantine city, Moscow was regarded as the center of the Eastern church.

It was believed that God had established four empires that would succeed one another: Babylon, Persia, Macedonia, and Rome, and that during the Roman Empire, Christ would return to earth. But Rome had become heretical, and Byzantium had cooperated with the papacy, so Moscow would be the center of Christendom and be forever.

The "forever" part was important to the faithful, because Russia was surrounded by enemies. To the west were the Swedes, Poles, and Germans. Elsewhere the Tatars threatened, exacting tribute from Russia. Alexander Nevsky finally fought off the Swedes in 1240, but the church regarded him as a saint because of his humble dealing with the dreaded Tatars, and not for his military victory. The Tatars menaced and intimidated (and at times ruled large parts of) Russia until the reign of Ivan III (the Great), who defeated them in 1480.

You may recall that the East and the West differed in the practice of the sacraments, but not in their number. The East also differed in the distribution of the Lord's Supper. A broken piece of the consecrated bread was dipped into the cup of blessed wine and given to the communicants, including baptized and anointed infants, on a spoon. The practice was called "intinction."

The Russian church looked with disdain on Western Christianity, because it regarded the many and frequent changes as a sign that its own unchanging orthodoxy deserved the title of the Holy Orthodox Church. Doing good—not fasting and monasticism—it was held, gains eternal life. The liturgy (divine service) was a dramatization of the life of Christ. Chants without instrumental accompaniment constituted the musical part of the liturgy. Priests were allowed to marry, but if their wives died they were not permitted to remarry; this was based on an interpretation of **1 Timothy 3:2 ("the husband of but one wife").**

The highest virtues were regarded to be humility, according to the Beatitudes, and self-sacrifice for the common good. The whole nation was perceived to be a family, with the czar as its head. Even strangers were addressed as "uncle" or "brother."

Orthodox worshipers kneel or stand; there are no pews. Unlike the Western services, people come and go throughout the lengthy liturgy.

In Orthodox theology every person bears the image of God; people inherit the corruption and mortality of Adam but not his guilt; salvation must be earned (faith plus works are necessary); Jesus changed the result of Adam's disobedience; and Christ's crucifixion and resurrection are regarded as a single action in which His victory is revealed.

The Orthodox church teaches that those who die in the faith are still members of God's family; therefore the living are to pray for the departed and ask the departed to pray for them. Mary is venerated as *theotokos* (the one who gave birth to God). She is ever-virgin and pure in that she committed no actual sin. They do not hold the later Western teachings about Mary.

Devotional life includes veneration of the icons of the Trinity and the saints. The Orthodox make a distinction between the worship of God, the veneration of Mary, and the veneration of saints, relics, and icons.

Sometime around 1880 Russian students who had attended German schools brought home the teachings of Karl Marx. After the famous revolution in November 1917, Lenin, exiled leader of the Bolshevik (Communist) Party, returned to Russia and gained control of the government. In two months the ancient close relation between church and state came to an end. Church property was confiscated, although the church was allowed to exist as a cultural group.

But even the toleration of the church ended in 1922. The government prohibited images, religious funerals and processions, and the observance of Sunday. A few years later, teachers were bound to take an oath that they opposed Christianity, and people under the age of 18 were not allowed to attend religious services. The theory was to let the older generation of believers die out and so Christianity would fade away entirely.

FOR DISCUSSION

1. Define *Renaissance*. What aspects were contrary to Christianity? Explain.
2. What positive things came out of the Renaissance?
3. How can we say that God was in control when the popes lived such immoral lives?
4. Sometimes the immorality today causes us to shake our heads in despair. What is a better way to approach such a problem?
5. Why did the East regard itself as superior to the West?
6. Give examples of people who resist change. Which of these people do you admire? Why? Which ones do you look down upon? Why?
7. What evidences of "Renaissance" do you find in the world today? How do they affect the church and its members?

A WORD FROM THE WORD

You, O Lord, sit enthroned forever; Your renown endures through all generations. You will arise and have compassion on Zion, for it is time to show favor to her; the appointed time has come.
Psalm 102:12–13

SESSION 10

Concluding Activities for Unit 1

TERMS AND PEOPLE

Write brief definitions of the terms and brief descriptions of the people that follow:
1. Gospel (strict sense)
2. Muhammad
3. Iconoclasm
4. Monasticism
5. Donation of Constantine
6. Richard the Lion-Hearted
7. Seven Sacraments
8. Scholasticism
9. William of Ockham
10. Renaissance
11. Leonardo da Vinci
12. Vladimir

SHORT ANSWER

Write a short answer to each of the following questions:
1. Why is the Gospel "the power of God"?
2. What were the positive and negative results of Augustine's *The City of God?*
3. Name the "five pillars of Islam."
4. What are some good uses of images in church or in religious ceremonies? How can images be abused?
5. In what way did the work of the monks benefit the church in years to come?
6. What claims did Pope Innocent III make regarding the authority of the papacy?
7. What common motive did the crusaders share with their opponents?
8. List the main causes of the schism between the Eastern and Western churches.
9. What was the main reason for the breakdown of papal power when Boniface VIII was pope?
10. What is meant by the "Babylonian Captivity of the Church"?
11. Identify the positive and the negative influences brought about by the Renaissance.
12. Name some of the differences between the practices of the Eastern and the Western church.

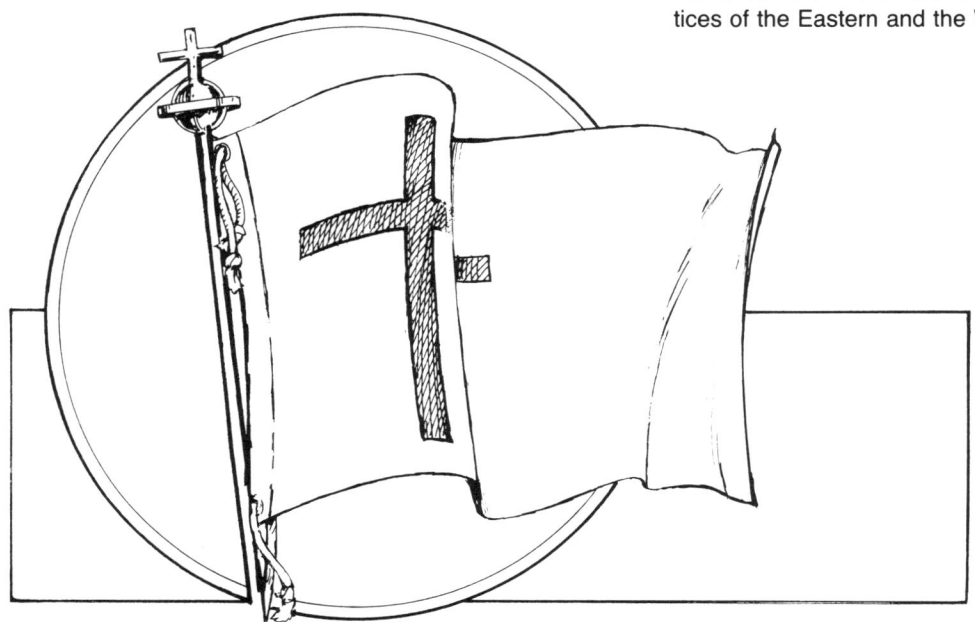

UNIT 2
The Reformation Era

There is a time for everything, and a season for every activity under heaven: . . . A time to plant and a time to uproot . . . . He has made everything beautiful in its time. He has also set eternity in the hearts of men; yet they cannot fathom what God has done from beginning to end.

Ecclesiastes 3:1–2, 11

"I'll sue!"

This is what 1 of every 15 Americans threatened and did in 1986. As Chief Justice Warren Burger of the Supreme Court put it, litigation has become "a way to solve all problems." The amount of individual awards is also rapidly becoming larger. Only one lawsuit for $1 million occurred in 1962; two years later more than 400 judgments involving that amount were made, and the number has continued to grow during the ensuing years.

We have seen how threats by those in power both in and out of the church gradually became meaningless; a spirit of independence and nationalism gave people courage to defy church authority. Had this not happened, would Luther and the other Reformers been as bold as they were? Or do threats provoke people to action?

In any event, God had prepared the world for a time of change. The press, communications, the political structure, industry, the arts, and science were "right." God would work with people in the church to uproot religious beliefs and practices that had no support in Scripture, and to plant the good seed. This happened in the era called the Reformation. It was spearheaded by the son of a German miner.

SESSION 11

Luther's Early Life

... a time to be born.

Ecclesiastes 3:2

Martin Luther was born November 10, 1483, in Eisleben, Germany, and was baptized the following (St. Martin's) day. During the next year his parents, Hans and Margarethe Luder (the family name was spelled several ways) moved to Mansfield, which was located in a productive mining region. By the time Martin was 8, his ambitious and hardworking father had already become one of the community's leading citizens.

Contrary to what many believe, Hans Luder was not poor, for it took money to give his young son a quality education. Possibly the poverty stories are valid if they hark back to the earlier days of his parents' life.

Also exaggerated at times are the accounts of the harsh punishment young Martin endured in his childhood. Children were punished with spankings in order to correct them, as they were in our country a generation or so ago. "Grounding" them or forbidding them certain privileges was unheard of. Paddlings were indeed administered in the schools, but if they became too severe, parents could take their children out of school.

From the beginning Martin's parents assumed that he would be so educated that advanced learning would lead him to a respectable profession. At Mansfield he learned grammar, logic, and rhetoric, all prerequisites for higher schools. Latin received a great deal of attention; in later years he demonstrated proficiency in handling the Vulgate (the Latin translation of the Bible). The Mansfield school also offered considerable instruction in religion. Students learned the Ten Commandments, the Creed, the Our Father, the Confession of Sins, and the Hail Mary. Parts of the Mass were memorized, including versicles (sentences embracing the psalms and canticles), psalms, hymns, and prayers.

Perhaps Luther's interest in music developed at Mansfield. Students learned the psalm tones and were taught the basics of harmony. Considerable time was given to a study of the *pericopes* (pe-RIC-o-peez)—the Epistles and Gospels assigned to the various feasts and festivals. Though Luther later complained about the heavy "law" content of these selections, he certainly was exposed to God's Word before his monastic experience.

When he was 14, Martin was sent to Magdeburg, where he received instruction from members of the Brethren of the Common Life, who, as we learned in session 9, did not oppose the organized church but quietly worked for reform through the education of the young. The Brethren encouraged devotional reading and stressed the importance of attending church services.

It is likely that Luther was exposed to the Bible during this year, as the Brethren emphasized the reading of the Scriptures. You may have heard it said that the Bible was chained in order to keep people from reading it. But what we today know as bookcases did not exist in those days, and, therefore, valuable books were chained to prevent careless readers from misplacing or losing them.

At 18, Martin entered the University of Erfurt, a school regarded as the best of all the German universities, particularly in law and in the liberal arts. We know that Luther would enter the monastery four years later. Let us take a careful look at what transpired at Erfurt that led him to make the surprising move.

After enrolling in the department of liberal arts in the spring of 1501, Luther completed the work for his bachelor's degree (B. A.) by the end of 1502, ranking 30th in a class of 57. Continuing his studies, he went on to receive his master's degree (M. A.) early in 1505, this time ranking 2d in a class of 17. The degree gave him the right to teach in a liberal arts school, but he acceded to his father's wish and began studying law the following May. While he began the venture with a conscientious effort to do well, he quickly discovered that it simply did not interest him, and soon he was reading other literature.

Erfurt, an old university dating back to the 14th century, had an enrollment of some 2,000 students, who lived in dormitories designed like monasteries. Students seeking a degree were required to spend at least one year in the dormitory, closely supervised by an assigned faculty member. Final examinations for the degree were given only to students who were approved by the faculty member. If the student who was recommended was guilty of immoral behavior, the faculty member was punished and could lose his position.

The religious life in the dormitories resembled a monastery in several ways: daily prayer, Bible reading, and confession were a part of the operation. Women were not permitted to visit the dormitories. Students could mingle with women only at weddings and certain other celebrations, but they needed permission even for that privilege. Nor were students allowed to be out of the dormitories "after hours." Records showed where students spent time in the community, and expulsion could result if their behavior proved to be unsatisfactory.

To the astonishment of friends and family, Luther requested to be admitted to the Erfurt Augustine Order on July 17, 1505. Perhaps you know the "flash of lightning" story. Two weeks before he announced the decision, Luther was thrown to the ground by a lightning flash during a heavy storm as he returned to Erfurt from his home. He called on St. Ann and made a vow that he would enter the monastery if his life was spared. Luther's father was furious, and his friends whom he joined for a farewell dinner were shocked.

Two earlier incidents—an accident in which he severed a vein with his sword, and the sudden death of a friend—may have influenced Martin to enter the monastery.

Not all historians agree with the above reasons for Luther's action. Some maintain that he lived the life of an average student in those days, and the decision was as much a bolt out of the blue as the lightning experience that caused it.

A third school concludes that the decision would have been eventually made even without the thunderstorm. In his *Der Junge Luther,* Heinrich Boehmer favors the explanation of this group:

"We may safely conclude that in that moment of great nervous tension a decision, long prepared by the inner battles of recent months but up to then held back by doubt and reflection of various kinds, suddenly broke through. For Luther was one of those men to whom seemingly sudden decisions come only after long bitter struggle and break through abruptly in a moment of tense excitement. We can, therefore, safely claim that inwardly he was already on the road to the monastery when the lightning at Stotternheim crashed down upon him. The hysterical fear that came over him in that moment only hastened the decision; it did not create the attitude of mind out of which the decision was made" (Quoted by E. G. Schwiebert in *Luther and His Times,* p. 144).

FOR DISCUSSION

1. Parents often want their children to "do better than they did," so they work hard in order to provide them with a better education than they themselves had. In your opinion, is this an admirable motive? Why or why not?
2. Why was Luther's training in Latin helpful to him in years to come?
3. Do you think Luther appreciated his study of Latin? How do you motivate yourself to study something (history, math, etc.) you do not seem to need?
4. How might the teachings of the members of the Brethren of the Common Life have influenced Luther's later efforts to reform the church?
5. Think of the "mentors" you have had. Who is (was) your favorite? Why? How many *good* teachers does one need in a lifetime?
6. Luther's father was determined that he study law. Is it advisable for a parent to decide on his child's future? Defend your opinion.
7. Name a few of the events that caused Luther to enter the monastery.

A WORD FROM THE WORD

One thing I ask of the Lord, this is what I seek: that I may dwell in the house of the Lord all the days of my life, to gaze upon the beauty of the Lord and to seek Him in His temple. For in the day of trouble He will keep me safe in His dwelling; He will hide me in the shelter of His tabernacle and set me high upon a rock.

Psalm 27:4–5

SESSION 12

Luther: Monk and Priest

... a time to be silent.
Ecclesiastes 3:7

LUTHER'S INITIATION

After he prostrated himself before the prior of the monastery, Luther was asked what he desired. He said he desired God's grace and mercy. He then got to his feet and was further questioned about his marital status, his attachments, and whether or not he had a disease. When these were answered in the negative, the prior told him about the hardships he would experience as a member of the order. Martin exchanged his street dress for the habit of a monk, a black cloak worn over a simple white garment.

After some of Martin's hair was cut and a part of the head shaved, he was given a small black skullcap that he wore even in the privacy of his cell. This room, about 7 by 10 feet, was furnished with a straw bed, table, and chair. Unheated, the room had one window that faced a cemetery and a door that could not be locked from the inside. No talking was allowed in the halls. Besides participating in the recitation of the canonical hours, Luther was told to walk with downcast eyes and given instruction on how to conduct himself at meals.

LUTHER THE PRIEST

Luther was consecrated a priest in 1507. In saying his first mass, he was fearful of making a mistake. To add to his concerns, his father attended the meal given in honor of the new priest. Old Hans reminded all present that the Scriptures demand that we should "honor father and mother." Luther's later writings indicated that the appeal to Scripture made an impression on him.

After his first mass, Luther's inner conflict seemed to increase. He doubted that leading the monastic life of self-denial, keeping the rules of the order, and further study would ever assure him of salvation. Keenly aware of his weaknesses, he did receive some comfort from John Staupitz, vicar-general of the German Augustinians, who urged him to look to a gracious Savior: "First find yourself in the wounds of Christ."

LUTHER VISITS ROME

In the winter of 1510 an older monk was sent to Rome to oppose a plan that would unite two factions in his order of monks. Martin accompanied him, as the order would not permit its members to travel alone. Since the journey from Erfurt to Rome took over a month, hundreds of monasteries throughout Europe offered welcome relief to weary travelers. Once in Italy, Luther was impressed with the manners and dress of its citizens, but did not take kindly to their anticlerical attitude and their lack of respect for sacred things. The answer to the appeal regarding the proposed union was delayed for a month. This gave Luther and his associate time to see Rome.

At that time the city had a population of about 40,000. It was a blend of splendor and decay: 70 monasteries, many of which were not operating, especially those of the Benedictines; church buildings and other ancient ruins; narrow, dirty streets in the heart of the city; and palaces of cardinals.

The two made the customary pilgrimage to the seven major churches. Confession was first said, and Communion was received at the end of the journeys, so the pilgrims were bound to fast along the way.

Luther must have been disappointed in the results: he had no more peace of mind than before. In fact, he was saddened by the manner in which masses were said—hurried and without paying attention to what was said. Church services were incomplete, despite the large number of priests and other clerics. Sermons were delivered only during the penitential seasons, and the sacraments were often not dispensed even on festive days.

A part of the problem Luther alluded to, the manner in which masses were read (it reminded him of a juggling act) existed because many priests simply did not know Latin.

In the German community of Rome he heard about the corruption in the papal court—about Alexander VI and his illegitimate children and about the present pope, Julius II, who often engaged in all manner of extracurricular activities.

A vast number of "relics" attracted the pilgrims. Included were thorns from the crown that Christ had worn, some of the Virgin Mary's hair, Pilate's inscription on the cross, pieces of the cross, pieces of the loaves of bread with which Jesus had fed the 5,000, pieces of silver that Judas had received when he betrayed Jesus, and even the rod that Moses used when he struck the rock that gave water to the thirsty Israelites!

LUTHER EARNS THE TITLE OF DOCTOR

John Staupitz, who wanted Luther to succeed him as professor of exegesis (Bible interpretation), sent Luther to Erfurt so that he might finish his work and obtain a doctorate in theology. Luther was successful in this (1512) and eventually took Staupitz' place at the University of Wittenberg. He remained at that post until he died. Although he was now a Doctor of Theology, he still continued the struggle to please an angry God.

Luther's duties multiplied. Besides lecturing twice a week, he became the official preacher at the Black Cloister and soon began preaching in the town church. Staupitz appointed him a district vicar, making him responsible for the well-being of 10 convents. As he gave lectures on the psalms in 1514 and the following year, the conversion of Martin Luther took place. This is how he described it:

In the meantime in the same year (1519) I had begun again to lecture on the Psalter, believing that with my classroom experience in lecturing on the Psalms and the Letters of Paul to the Romans, Galatians, and Hebrews, I was now better prepared. All the while I was absorbed with the passionate desire to get better acquainted with the author of Romans. Not that I did not succeed, as I had resolved, in penetrating more deeply into the subject in my investigation, but I stumbled over the words (chapter 1:17) concerning "the righteousness of God revealed in the Gospel." For the concept "God's righteousness" was repulsive to me, as I was accustomed to interpret it according to scholastic philosophy, namely, as the "formal or active" righteousness, in which God proves Himself righteous in that He punishes the sinner as an unrighteous person . . . until, after days and nights of wrestling with the problem, God finally took pity on me, so that I was able to comprehend the inner connection between the two expressions, "The righteousness of God is revealed in the Gospel" and "The just shall live by faith."

Then I began to comprehend the "righteousness of God" through which the righteous are saved by God's grace, namely, through faith; that the "righteousness of God" which is revealed through the Gospel was to be understood in a passive sense in which God through mercy justifies man by faith, as it is written, "The just shall live by faith." Now I felt exactly as though I had been born again, and I believed that I had entered Paradise through widely opened doors. I then went through the Holy Scriptures as far as I could recall them from memory, and I found in other parts the same sense: the "work of God" is that which He works in us, the "strength of God" is that through which He makes us strong, the "wisdom of God" is that through which He makes us wise, and so the "power of God," the "blessing of God," and the "honor of God" are likewise to be interpreted.

As violently as I had formerly hated the expression "righteousness of God," so I was now as violently compelled to embrace the new conception of grace and, thus, for me, the expression of the Apostle really opened the Gates of Paradise.

(From Luther's preface to the Latin edition of his "Opera Latina I," published in 1545, quoted by E. G. Schwiebert in *Luther and His Times*, pp. 285–86.)

Luther became popular both in the classroom and in the pulpit. He had the ability to reduce technical terms to the language of the people, making use of the German language when doing it. Students greatly appreciated his lectures because they were founded on the Scriptures rather than on the theology and philosophy of scholasticism.

FOR DISCUSSION

1. What moved Luther to take up the austere life of a monk?
2. What disappointments did Luther experience after he said his first mass?
3. How did the visit to Rome only add to his inner struggle?
4. Why did Luther "violently hate" the expression, the "righteousness of God"?
5. Luther was shocked at the behavior of the clergy in Rome. Would your personal faith suffer if your pastor or some other respected church leader were caught in a scandal? How would you respond to such a situation?

A WORD FROM THE WORD

You turned my wailing into dancing; You removed my sackcloth and clothed me with joy, that my heart may sing to You and not be silent. O Lord my God, I will give You thanks forever.

Psalm 30:11–12

SESSION 13

Indulgences and Theses

. . . a time to search.
Ecclesiastes 3:6

INDULGENCES

As we learned in session 8, the sale of indulgences was based on the notion that Christ and the saints did good works beyond God's demands and that these good works could be bought from the church to atone for the sins of the living and the dead. Originally, at the time of the Crusades, it was taught that Christians who died in battle against the Muslims were absolved of their sins and thus delivered from temporal punishment and suffering in purgatory.

Because everyone could not be personally involved in a crusade, a new arrangement enabled them to pay the church the cost of sending a soldier and so receive absolution. By Luther's day, even contrition was unnecessary, and the simple purchase of indulgences procured the forgiveness of sins.

Eventually people could buy an elaborate letter of indulgence with papal signatures and seals. It gave written assurance of entry into heaven. Sales skyrocketed. The money, it was claimed, was needed to finish the magnificent St. Peter's Church building. So Leo X (pope 1513–21) promoted the indulgence traffic. Countries in western Europe resisted the effort, but it was permitted in Germany.

The sale became a personal matter with Luther when Johann Tetzel, a Dominican monk from Leipzig, was peddling indulgences in the towns of Zerbst and Jueterbock, which were close to Wittenberg. When Luther asked some of his parishioners to repent and mend their sinful ways, they confronted him with the Indulgence letters they had obtained. An eyewitness account of the sales reads:

"In those days indulgences were so much respected that when an indulgence agent was brought to town, the papal bull was carried on a velvet or gold cloth, while all the priests, monks, councilmen, teachers, students, men, women, girls, and children met him carrying flags and candles and singing while they marched in procession. Meanwhile all the bells in town rang, and as the procession entered the church, the organ played. A red cross was placed in the middle of the church on which the papal papers were hung, etc.; in brief, one could not have received and entertained God in a more impressive fashion than this."
(From Myconius' *Historia Reformationis,* quoted by E. G. Schwiebert, *Luther and His Times,* p. 310.)

Three services were conducted before the sales took place. The first was held in the town square, or center, where Tetzel preached about the horrible suffering of the damned in hell. The second, which took place in the largest church, featured Tetzel speaking about purgatory. He described the misery of the parents of many in attendance. In the third sermon he discoursed on the great differences between the damned in hell and the saved in heaven. As people then came forward to buy indulgences, their financial situation was reviewed. The wealthier were required to pay up to $300, while the destitute received indulgences only for the asking.

Precisely a year before Luther nailed the 95 Theses to a door of the Castle Church in Wittenberg, he preached a sermon about the proper use of indulgences. Genuine contrition, he said, should be lifelong for a Christian, and punishment should not be something to be evaded. In a stronger sermon four months later he warned that indulgences allow people to sin.

A copy of the indulgence salesman's instruction book fell into Luther's hands the following October, and he decided to discuss the issue with other faculty members who were willing to do so. As was the custom, he nailed the theses for discussion on a church door, October 31, 1517. This marked the beginning of the Reformation.

The timing was just right: pilgrims had gathered in Wittenberg to view the 17,000 relics at the church on All Saints Day (November 1) and to receive indulgences when they prayed before them. Still, Luther did not intend to stir up the populace, otherwise he would have written the theses in German, not Latin. They were not written to "reform the church" nor were they his last word on doctrinal matters. It was a time to search out God's truth.

As one writer put it, the sounds of the hammer echoed throughout the world. Within a month copies of the theses were all over Europe.

THE 95 THESES

Luther's very first thesis summarized his thrust against indulgences: "When our Lord and Master Jesus Christ said, 'Repent,' He willed the entire life of believers to be one of repentance." Rather than the nonexistent "treasury of merits" which could be bought for money, he declared that "the true treasure of the church is the most holy gospel of the glory and grace of God" (Thesis 62).

Luther did not attack the papacy and other offices of the church, nor did he bitterly protest against the sacraments. But he did distinguish between true repentance (the attitude of a contrite sinner) and penance (the formal, sacramental act). A truly contrite sinner does not seek to escape from punishment by indulgences, but accepts it in humility. While respecting and even defending the papal office—he believed that the practice of selling indulgences had a negative effect on the papacy—he maintained that the pope could not remit punishment. Every Christian receives the benefits of Jesus Christ; we do not need an indulgence letter.

Luther did have questions: Why didn't the pope out of holy love deliver the souls from purgatory? With all his wealth why didn't the pope build St. Peter's? Why did the penitent have to pay money before sins were forgiven?

REACTION TO THE THESES

An advisor to the pope accused Luther of heresy. Luther explained the theses in "Resolutions Concerning the Virtue of Indulgences," dedicated to the pope. (He did not believe that Tetzel worked with papal approval.) While Luther stated that his views were not contrary to the Scriptures or the church, he suggested that even church councils could err. He sent a copy of the "Resolutions" to the pope and reaffirmed him to be the minister and servant of the keys.

The distribution of the theses practically ended the sale of indulgences, so Leo X first tried to put pressure on Luther through the Augustinian Order. He appeared before the general chapter of the Saxon province at Heidelberg in April 1518, but this only added fuel to the fire, as he made a brilliant defense of his views and won many followers.

With the Dominicans pushing hard, the pope ordered Luther to appear in Rome. Fearing that he would be put to death in Rome and that the cause he championed would be lost, Luther asked Elector Frederick the Wise to intervene. For political reasons Leo agreed that a meeting between Cardinal Cajetan and Luther could be held in Augsburg. When asked to recant, he refused to do so unless he could be shown (by reason or the authority of Scripture, the church fathers, or even papal decrees) that he was wrong.

Finally, in 1521, Charles V (king of Spain as Charles I, 1516–56, and Holy Roman emperor, 1519–56), persuaded by Frederick that Luther be given a fair hearing, convened the Diet of Worms. Luther was asked if he was the author of a number of books that had been placed before him. He replied that he had written them but that some were missing. He was then asked if he would recant any part of them. Luther asked for time to consider and was given one day. The next day, April 18, 1521, as he stood before the most powerful assembly in Europe at that time, he said: "Unless I am convinced by the testimonies of the Holy Scriptures or evident reason (for I believe neither in the Pope nor councils alone, since it has been established that they have often erred and contradicted themselves), I am bound by the Scriptures adduced by me, and my conscience has been taken captive by the Word of God, and I am neither able nor willing to recant, since it is neither safe nor right to act against conscience. God help me. Amen."

FOR DISCUSSION

1. Why was the indulgence claim deceptive?
2. Why did Luther object to the sale of indulgences?
3. Describe how the sale of indulgences took place in a town. Compare them to the ways religious groups raise money today. What abuses, if any, do you see?
4. Why did Luther's theses spread so fast?
5. Discuss the role of economics in the pope's practice of selling indulgences. Give a current example of economics causing a person, church, or government to conduct an "evil" practice.
6. Why did Luther's theses cause such a dramatic drop in the sales of indulgences?
7. Luther stood firm in his faith in the face of possible death. Give examples of people you know who have shown the same kind of faithfulness. How could they withstand the temptations to compromise their faith? Where do we get such power?

A WORD FROM THE WORD

My zeal wears me out, for my enemies ignore Your words. Your promises have been thoroughly tested, and Your servant loves them. Though I am lowly and despised, I do not forget Your precepts. Your righteousness is everlasting and Your law is true.

Psalm 119:139–142

SESSION 14

Luther the Writer

. . . a time to speak.
Ecclesiastes 3:7

Luther knew the power of the printed word. This was demonstrated in the spread of the 95 Theses. The time to be silent at the monastery and the time to search at the university were over. It was a time to speak, and to speak boldly.

LUTHER'S HYMNS

Someone has said that the Reformation was sung into the hearts of the people and that his opponents dreaded the hymns Luther wrote more than his sermons. It is not certain whether he wrote hymns throughout his whole life, or mostly in 1523 and 1524 (which hardly seems likely). In either case, 24 hymns ascribed to Luther were included in Johann Walther's hymnal, which was published 1524. He wrote both the words and the music for his best-known work, "A Mighty Fortress," which is included even in Catholic worship books today. Other popular hymns are: "We All Believe in One True God" (a metrical version of the creed); "Isaiah, Mighty Seer"; "From Heaven Above"; and "Lord, Keep Us Steadfast." The robust quality of these stanzas has stood the test of time. Twenty-five of Luther's hymns appear in *Lutheran Worship.*

Luther retained the order of the Mass, but he deleted the parts having to do with sacrifice and work-righteousness connected with the Words of Institution. He also prepared a simple "German Mass" with the hope that, in time, worship would be expressed in the language of the people. Hymn stanzas were substituted for chants and other liturgical sections (see *Lutheran Worship,* pages 197–98).

TRANSLATION OF THE BIBLE

After the Diet of Worms, Luther was given safe conduct back to Wittenberg, but then he would be an "outlaw." Anyone could expect to be rewarded for capturing him and turning him over to state authorities. One of his friends "captured" him and spirited him away to Wartburg, dressed as a knight. He grew a beard (lest he be recognized) and spent 10 months in the huge fortress.

There he translated the New Testament from Greek into German. Completed in September 1522 and published that same month, 5,000 copies were sold before the end of the year. An estimated 200,000 copies were sold during the following 12 years. The translation of the Old Testament was finished in February 1541, but Luther kept revising it until the time of his death. The difficulties of the task were echoed in the following words of Luther:

"We are now sweating over the translation of the Prophets into German. O God, what a great and hard toil it requires to compel the writers against their will to speak German! They do not want to give up their Hebrew and imitate the barbaric German. Just as though a nightingale should be compelled to imitate a cuckoo and give up her glorious melody, even though she hates a song in monotone" (Translation by Reu, *Luther's German Bible,* quoted by E. G. Schwiebert, *Luther and His Times,* page 647).

THE SMALL CATECHISM

This little volume written by Luther (1529) is the oldest book of instruction of its kind, in any subject, that is still in use. It was sorely needed, as Luther points out in the Preface, because not only the common people, but even priests and other teachers were "quite incompetent and unfitted" to impart the chief teachings of the Bible.

However, it was intended not only for the classroom but also for the home. Each section begins with, "As the Head of the Family Should Teach Them (It) in a Simple Way to His Household." Through the ensuing years the section entitled "Confession" or "The Office of the Keys" appears in various places in relation to the other chief parts. The questions in the Office of the Keys were not written by Luther, but were added later. They are in agreement with his teachings.

THE AUGSBURG CONFESSION AND THE APOLOGY

Virtually every Lutheran church body accepts the Augsburg Confession as a statement of faith. It came into being when Emperor Charles V convened a meeting (a "diet") of representatives of free cities throughout the empire (June 1530) in order to unite the nation before his forthcoming war against the Turks.

When Charles entered the city, he was royally greeted by the gathering of princes, other notables, and the townspeople. On the morning of the Corpus Christi (Body of Christ) festival (June 16), the host (consecrated bread) was paraded through the city. Charles marched behind it, along with supporters of Rome, but the "Lutheran" representatives refused to participate. As documents were being readied, Charles tried to be neutral. Philipp Melanchthon, one of Luther's co-reformers, drew up the summary statements of the Wittenberg theologians, because Luther was unable to be present, being under the ban of both pope and emperor.

Finally, by June 24 the time had come to review the work of Melanchthon, whose co-workers insisted on a public reading of the document, but an argument as to whether it should be read in Latin or in German delayed proceedings. Because the meeting was being held on German soil, it was decided to read it in that language. Time ran out, so it was postponed to the next day. On June 25 about three in the afternoon the historic moment arrived. People filled the meeting room and the surrounding courtyard. The event is described as follows:

"At the Diet of Augsburg the Evangelical Confession prepared by Philip Melanchthon and approved by Elector John and other princes and estates alike, written in both Latin and German, was read in German by the Chancellor of Electoral Saxony, Doctor Christian Beyer, in the so-called Bishop's Court so loudly and distinctly that not only the assembled Emperor, Electors, and estates, before which he spoke, could hear it, but also outside in front of the room and even in the Palatinate and the Castle Court they could understand every word. The reading took two hours. After the reading Doctor Gregorius Pontanus took from Doctor Beyer the German text, which had been read, and gave it with the Latin copy, which he already had, to the imperial secretary, Alexander Schweiss, from whom the Kaiser took the Latin copy" (From *Annales*, by J. S. Mueller [1700], quoted by E. G. Schwiebert in *Luther and His Times*, p. 729).

After this the Romanists prepared a "Confutation" (Refutation), which they read on August 3. Charles insisted that the Lutheran position be forsaken, but its adherents refused to do so. By September 22, Melanchthon completed an answer (Apology) to the Confutation, but the emperor declined to have it read. On the same day he called a recess to the proceedings with the assurance that he would ask the pope to convene a general church council to resolve the issues. So ended one of the most historic meetings in the annals of Christianity.

Melanchthon reworked the Apology, and it was printed the following spring. It covers the same ground as the Augsburg Confession but is much longer. It is one of the official confessional documents of the Lutheran church.

The Augsburg Confession and the Apology do not touch on certain issues previously raised by Luther, such as purgatory and transubstantiation. Obviously, efforts had been made to appease the opponents and to demonstrate how the Lutherans were in agreement with Rome regarding the errors of the Anabaptists, Pelagians, Donatists, and Novatians. But even these concessions did not convince the Roman Catholics.

FOR DISCUSSION

1. Compare two of Luther's hymns with two other hymns that are popular among Christians today. What differences do you find? what similarities?
2. Show what a remarkable task was accomplished with the speedy translation and printing of the New Testament. (Compare with work you have done or that you know about.) Why was Luther able to do this? Why were the sales so high?
3. What reasons can you give someone to encourage that person to read the Bible every day? Develop a Bible-reading plan that fits your schedule.
4. You probably already were familiar with the Small Catechism. What new fact did you learn about it in this session?
5. Suppose that you have both the Augsburg Confession and Luther's Small Catechism on your shelf. Give an example of a time you would choose the Augsburg Confession to find the answer to a question. When would you choose the Small Catechism?
6. Compare the practice of confession as described in the Augsburg Confession with practices of confession today.
7. Why did Charles V want to unify the people of his empire?

A WORD FROM THE WORD

Do not snatch the word of truth from my mouth, for I have put my hope in Your laws. I will always obey Your law, for ever and ever. I will walk about in freedom, for I have sought out Your precepts. I will speak of Your statutes before kings and will not be put to shame.

Psalm 119:43–46

SESSION 15

Other Reformers

. . . a time for war and a time for peace.
Ecclesiastes 3:8

The Reformation, designed to bring about a wholesome cleansing of the church, gave impetus to the emergence of leaders with various theological, political, and economic views.

SOMETHING THEY AGREED ABOUT!

We have been reading about differences between the Roman and Lutheran churches. Leaders of both churches agreed, however, that those reformers who denied that the sacraments are a means of grace and who injected human reason and feelings into their religious views were teaching error.

THE ANABAPTISTS

Even among themselves such radical reformers had differences, but they agreed on at least three beliefs:

—direct revelations from the Holy Spirit took precedence over the written Word and the sacraments;

—existing churches should be shunned, because too many unbelievers belonged to those congregations;

—infant baptism was not valid.

Those reformers did not agree, however, on how to conduct themselves in society. Some passively resisted the authorities, refusing to take up arms or serve in a civil office. Others held that a true believer must work to destroy existing authorities and usher in the kingdom of God on earth.

Did these groups come into being because of Luther's teachings? No doubt they were encouraged by the new freedom he espoused. Justification by faith alone diminished the importance of a highly organized church; the universal priesthood of all believers made the intermediary role of priests and bishops unnecessary; and many interpreted the freedom of those who believe the Gospel to mean freedom from human oppression. The downtrodden peasants especially were quick to identify with these views.

MUENZER AND THE REVOLUTION

One such radical reformer, Thomas Muenzer, advocated a violent overthrow of civil authorities, claiming that this was a result of visions, dreams, and direct revelations from God. In sermons based on **Deuteronomy 3,** he preached that the ungodly should be put to the sword; his battle cry was "Let not the blood cool on your swords!" He wanted to establish a kingdom of true believers on earth in which all possessions would be held in common.

Muenzer's followers took him at his word. In the summer of 1524 the Peasants' War broke out. In central Germany more than 40 castles and monasteries were destroyed. The revolt spread quickly because the German armies were at war in Italy.

Elsewhere peasants tried to bring about reform through peaceful negotiations. One group presented the Twelve Articles of the Swabian Peasants to Frederick the Wise, Luther, and Melanchthon (recognized leaders of the Reformation). They called for the right to choose their own pastors; the abolition of the lesser tithes; and the right to fish, hunt, and cut wood in common forests. They demanded an end to the seizure of common lands without fair payment and to the inheritance tax that took advantage of widows and orphans.

Early in 1525 the German soldiers began to return from Italy, and the princes unleashed their military forces against the peasants. Muenzer was captured and beheaded. In the end, the peasants were the losers: thousands were brutally slain, and those who survived had virtually everything taken from them. Defeated and disillusioned, many of them became indifferent to Lutheranism.

Nor did Luther's personal intervention help. His pamphlet *Admonition to Peace in Response to the Twelve Articles* came out too late, and his *Against the Murdering Hordes of Peasants* called on the princes to suppress revolt with the sword, and so it further alienated the peasants.

THE PEACE-LOVING MENNONITES

While sharing certain religious views of Muenzer, such as Anabaptism (from the Greek word for "baptizing again," a teaching that rejected the validity of infant baptism), Konrad Grebel (ca. 1498–1526) founded a movement that eventually gained respectability. He did not believe that people are born into the church, but become members by professing their faith and promising to lead a godly life. Grebel rejected the doctrine of the invisible church, taught that baptism only signified rebirth, and viewed the Lord's Supper as a meal of fellowship and remembrance that only signified a union with Christ and other true believers. It was celebrated in homes rather than in churches and, following the example of Christ, only in the evening.

These Anabaptists practiced nonresistance in times of oppression and persecution. Striving to be separate from the world, they refused either to assist the state in taking up arms or to hold a civil office.

During the time of Menno Simons (ca. 1492–1559) the Anabaptists, in spite of savage persecution, became widespread. Simons was a former Roman Catholic priest who traveled throughout Europe, preaching to the disillusioned peasants and others. He organized the Mennonite Church, which endorsed

—denial of original sin;
—personal conversion sealed by adult baptism;
—refusal to take up arms, take an oath, or hold civil office;
—avoidance of worldly pleasures;
—obedience to civil authorities unless their rules were contrary to God's Word and the conscience; and
—the practice of foot washing according to **John 13.**

Mennonites did not regard the sacraments to be important. Quakers and Baptists in later years accepted many of the Anabaptist-Mennonite beliefs.

THE LIBERTINES

The Libertine sect arose about 1529. They preferred "spiritual marriages" (which they said were not binding) to civil marriages. They did not view the Bible as God's Word and rejected the existence of angels and the devil. To them, nothing was truly bad, so sin was but an illusion, and salvation was the realization of these facts. They saw the events in the life, death, and resurrection of Christ as symbolic, not to be taken literally.

THE SOCINIANS, OR UNITARIANS

The last of the extremist groups, the Socinians, drew their beliefs from false teachings that went back to the early centuries of Christianity, when the doctrine of the Trinity and the deity of Christ were rejected.

Heading this sect was Fausto Sozzini, an Italian lawyer who left Italy in 1547 and began a Unitarian fellowship called the Polish Brethren. Their synod in 1603 agreed that a second baptism was not necessary if a person wanted to join their fellowship. The Socinians, or Unitarians, held to some supernatural beliefs (unlike those of today). They acknowledged the value of the New Testament, but denied the existence of hell, original sin and guilt, the Christian doctrine of the Trinity, the deity of Christ, and predestination. Salvation, they taught, has nothing to do with atonement for sin, but comes from the natural worth and dignity of people who are correctly instructed.

FOR DISCUSSION

1. What teachings of Luther most likely prompted the peasants to revolt?
2. What were the motives for the Peasants' War?
3. Probably some people saw the Reformation more as a political movement than a religious movement. Show that the same kind of thinking still occurs today—that people still confuse theology with politics, economics, or social issues.
4. Do you think the Peasants' Twelve Articles were unfair? Defend your answer.
5. How did politics, rather than theology, cause people to leave the Lutheran church during and after the Peasants' War? What nontheological issues threaten to divide the church today?
6. Compare the theology of Grebel with that of Scripture.
7. How did the Mennonites differ from those who followed Muenzer?
8. Which teachings of the Libertines are held by Christian Science today? Which teachings of the Unitarians are held today?
9. How would you respond to friends or acquaintances who claim they have direct revelations from God?

A WORD FROM THE WORD

Come and see the works of the Lord, the desolations He has brought on the earth. He makes wars cease to the ends of the earth; He breaks the bow and shatters the spear, He burns the shields with fire. "Be still, and know that I am God; I will be exalted among the nations, I will be exalted in the earth."

Psalm 46:8–10

SESSION 16

Luther and His Family

. . . a time to embrace.
Ecclesiastes 3:5

Was the life of Martin Luther just one battle after another? Was he forever fighting popes and peasants? Was he the kind of man you would want for a golfing partner? Was there one crisis after another, like some days in high school?

What did Luther look like? What kind of personality did he have? Why did he marry? What happened to his children? These are questions we ask about everyone, regardless of importance, but especially about a person who, even after four centuries, has an influence on our life and "in the life to come."

LUTHER'S PHYSICAL APPEARANCE

We need to rely on statements by his contemporaries and on portraits by Lucas Cranach to get a description of Luther, for photography had not yet been invented.

Like so many active men, Luther was rather thin, well up into his 30s. One of his contemporaries described him as skin and bones. Another, however, indicated that his bone structure was quite heavy. During Luther's middle-age years he became overweight.

A number of acquaintances told of the striking appearance of Luther's eyes. They were compared to the eyes of a falcon especially, but also like the eyes of a lion, burning like stars. Luther's opponents regarded his penetrating stare as evidence that he was possessed. God gave Luther a strong voice, an asset when he preached in the large churches.

LUTHER'S PERSONALITY

A childlike faith in the goodness of God accompanied the magnetic personality and other attributes. Because of this confidence, Luther was not afraid of man or devil.

Luther had a very active and creative mind. He often read the works of Augustine, Ockham, and Johann Tauler to gain a better understanding of God's Word, but he finally abandoned them and went to the Scriptures themselves. He obviously possessed a better-than-average memory, as his speedy outlay of many pamphlets and sermons testifies.

In spite of these necessary ingredients of scholarship, Luther was not aloof, distant, cold, or hard to get close to, like so many gifted people. Students loved to come to his study in the evening after attending his classes during the day. When he traveled to preach, Luther would be surrounded with ordinary people, comfortable in their presence just as he was at ease in the presence of princes and nobles. Because of his ongoing conversations with common people, his translation of the Bible was easily grasped. Away from the pulpit and outside the classroom, he would charm his various audiences with humor and wit.

LUTHER'S HEALTH

Yet, with all his seemingly unlimited energy and productivity, Luther (particularly in later years) did not enjoy good health. The severe disciplines of the Augustinian monks took their toll—and affected his disposition as well. He became very irritated over the troubles he encountered with Muenzer and other reformers who went too far and with the snail's-pace progress of the Reformation. The literature that Luther produced in later years often sharply denounced those who disagreed with him.

LUTHER'S MARRIAGE

In preparing for this session you read Article XXIII of the Augsburg Confession, which presents the Biblical view of marriage and a brief history of enforced celibacy. Already in 1520 Luther urged priests to take a bride if they so desired, and in the following year he encouraged monks to give it their consideration. Consequently, a number of his acquaintances took the step regardless of opposition. The convents were also affected. A dozen nuns (including Katharina von Bora) asked Luther to help them escape from the Marienthron Cloister and find husbands.

We cannot state positively how the nuns managed to sneak out of the cloister. It was a bold move; church law could require the death penalty for such violations.

Probably the story about the wagon and the barrels is correct. A man by the name of Leonhard Koppe, who lived in Torgau, made periodic trips to the cloister in a "covered" wagon and delivered barrels of fish. Somehow the nuns got on board and were safely and secretly delivered to Torgau, and then on to Wittenberg. There Luther tried to help them with money and prospective husbands. But Katharina was not willing to marry just anyone, and she rejected the pastor Luther chose for her. She did indicate, however, that she would marry Luther himself.

We do not know just how much of this Luther shared with his parents, but his father was pleased that he had left the monastery and was considering marriage. Luther and Katharina did not love each other at the beginning. Love was a result of married life rather than the cause of the union. Why, then, did they marry? Perhaps Luther felt that he should practice what he preached. Also, his bachelor days were chaotic when it came to regular meals and sleep. Possibly an earlier experience Katharina went through, a broken love affair in Wittenberg, may have prompted him to marry her out of pity.

LUTHER'S FAMILY

Katharina (Luther called her "my Rib," or "Katie," which is similar to the German word for "chain") was 26 and he was 42 when they were married on June 13, 1525. They were blessed with six children.

In addition to the companionship Katie gave to the sometimes lonely Reformer, she proved to be a good mother, housekeeper, and manager of the farms they owned.

By this time Martin Luther had become popular all over Germany. When the first child, Hans, was born and baptized, presents of all sorts poured into their home (the second floor of the Black Cloister). Within a few years the house echoed with the noise of children, happier sounds than the former somber chants of Augustinian monks at all hours of the night. But Martin and Katie also knew sorrow. Elizabeth, their second child, died less than a year after her birth.

Somehow Luther found time to spend with his children. His table talks (records of what he allegedly said at meals, transcribed by those eating with the Luthers) often made mention of what the children said and did. Other relatives lived with them: six children of a sister of Luther, six tutors for the children, and "Aunt Lena," who left the nunnery with Katie. In addition, a continuous flow of guests and poor clerics were all welcome—provided they joined in the family devotions. Singing, bowling, and chess balanced the hours of study and manual labor.

In years to come, Luther's children were provided for by the elector and the Mansfield princes. After studying law, Hans served in the court at Weimar. Martin studied theology, but did not occupy a pulpit. Paul became an able physician. Margaret married a member of a rich Prussian noble family. The other daughter's name was Magdalena ("little" Lena), and she died in her father's arms on Sept. 20, 1542, after he asked her if she was willing to go to her heavenly Father, to which she answered, "Yes, dear father, just as God wills." She was 13.

FOR DISCUSSION

1. In what way did God use Luther's personality to help the cause of the Reformation?
2. Why was Luther able to translate the Bible into the German language spoken by the people from day to day?
3. Name the factors that contributed to Luther's poor health as he became older.
4. Do you think Luther was a good manager of the body God gave him? Explain. What are some things you do to manage your body? How do you relate that management to **1 Corinthians 10:31?**
5. Describe how the marriage to Katharina von Bora benefited Luther.
6. Suppose two people who did not love each other would get married. How could that marriage "succeed"? How can any marriage "succeed"?

A WORD FROM THE WORD

Sons are a heritage from the Lord, children a reward from Him. Like arrows in the hands of a warrior are sons born in one's youth. Blessed is the man whose quiver is full of them.

Psalm 127:3–5

Blessed are all who fear the Lord, who walk in His ways. You will eat the fruit of your labor; blessings and prosperity will be yours. Your wife will be like a fruitful vine within your house; your sons will be like olive shoots around your table. Thus is the man blessed who fears the Lord.

Psalm 128:1–4

SESSION 17

Zwingli and Calvin

. . . a time to refrain.

Ecclesiastes 3:5

The Lord's Supper, which our Lutheran Confessions call "a true bond and union of Christians with Christ their Head and with one another," became (and still is) understood in different ways—ways that divide the visible church. Luther was joined in the Reformation by two other notable leaders, Ulrich Zwingli (1484–1531) and John Calvin (1509–64). A united Protestant movement might have been born if they could have reached agreement about the Lord's Supper.

ZWINGLI: EVERYTHING MUST GO

"All heresy flows, vents, and has its source therein that reason will master Holy Writ and turn it head over heels" (Luther, *Erlangen Ausgabe,* page 161). Certain leaders in the church, while encouraged because Luther placed Scripture above popes and councils, began to interpret the Word in such a way that it would be acceptable to human reason.

This was especially true of the Lord's Supper. First Karlstadt in Wittenberg, then Honius in the Netherlands, and finally Zwingli in Switzerland began to teach that Jesus' words, "This is My body" meant "This signifies My body." Karlstadt left Wittenberg after his unsuccessful attempt to reform the church. This led to a war of words between the Swiss reformers and the Wittenbergers. It came to a head at Marburg, Germany, on October 1–4, 1529, when the two groups met.

In spite of Luther's remark at the first meeting that the Swiss "have another spirit," they generally agreed on a number of teachings. They both rejected transubstantiation and the Mass as being a sacrifice.

However, they were sharply divided in their understanding of the body and blood of Christ in the Lord's Supper. Zwingli held that because Christ was at the right hand of God, His body and blood could not be on earth with the bread and wine. He claimed that the benefit of eating the bread and drinking the wine depended on how well the recipients meditated on Christ's suffering and death as they partook.

Thus, Zwingli tried to rationalize God by limiting Him to time and space. Luther believed that the same Christ who visited the disciples after the Resurrection when the doors were shut, and then disappeared from sight, could very well be "in, with, and under" the bread and wine in many places at the same time.

On the second day of the meeting Luther wrote the words *Hoc est corpus meum* ("This is My body") on the table in front of him, covering them with a cloth. As the argument went on, he later uncovered the words. Zwingli based his case on **John 6:63 ("the flesh counts for nothing"),** where Jesus was speaking of the spiritual eating and drinking of faith, not of the Lord's Supper. Another of the Swiss group claimed that **John 16** proved the absence of the body and blood. (Did not Christ say, they argued, He was returning to the Father so that the Spirit could be sent to them?)

In the end, Zwingli and his followers, despite the differences, asked the Lutherans if they would accept them as brothers. The Lutherans declined but indicated that they could be friends. It was a time to "refrain from embracing."

The Zwingli "spirit" was not only different in his rationalistic approach to Scripture interpretation, but also in his conception of what constituted Christian worship. He held that unless a practice was specifically prescribed in the New Testament, it had to be abolished. Pictures, statues, altars, candles, vestments, tapestry, and frescoes all had to go, which is exactly what happened in Zurich churches. Lutheran churches, however, retained everything except what was contrary to Scripture.

CALVIN: GOD IS SOVEREIGN!

John Calvin, a French reformer who was some 26 years younger than Luther and Zwingli, was also educated as a Catholic, but his career was in law (although his father first wanted him to be a priest). No later than 1533 he abandoned Catholicism and became a Protestant.

King Francis I of France persecuted the Protestants, accusing them of the Anabaptist teaching, of advocating overthrow of the government. In response to this Calvin published his *Institutes of the Christian Re-*

39

ligion, which became the most influential and famous manual of systematic theology produced during the Reformation. In it he defended the Protestants from the false accusations of the king and also showed that they were more faithful to the Scriptures and the Creed than were the Romanists.

Like Luther and Zwingli, Calvin accepted the Bible as the only rule of faith and life. The starting point of his theology was God's sovereign will and power. Humanity's greatest goal should be to further the glory of God on earth. He also taught that we could be saved only by the grace of God through the redemptive work of Christ. So far, so good, although Luther emphasized God's love more than His power and will.

In stressing God's will it followed that, according to Calvin, God had in eternity foreordained everything that would happen. Certain persons were ordained, or elected, to eternal life and certain others to eternal damnation (the doctrine of "double" or "absolute" predestination). So that the two sacraments would fit into the system, Calvin held that they were effective only for the elect. In Baptism the elect receive the forgiveness of sins; the nonelect do not. In the Lord's Supper the elect receive the body and blood in a "spiritual" but not in a physical way; the nonelect do not.

How can you be sure you belong to the elect? By cooperating with God's will and striving to be holy, said Calvin. This led to the idea that secular rulers should discipline their subjects according to the advice given by the leaders of the church.

In time the entire city of Geneva, Switzerland (where Calvin had gone to escape persecution), was so governed, as Calvinism became the successor to the Swiss Reformation under Zwingli. A consistory of 12 elders and 5 ministers ruled the community. People had to account for being absent from church services, having family quarrels, and playing cards. More serious crimes were punished with great severity. Fifty-eight persons were executed for adultery, blasphemy, heresy, and witchcraft between 1542 and 1546. Another 76 were banished from the city. Even so, Calvin's theology became widespread and was well received in much of Europe.

A SUMMARY STATEMENT

In order to explicate this controversy, it is necessary to mention, first of all, that there are two kinds of Sacramentarians. Some are crass Sacramentarians who set forth in clear German words what they believe in their hearts, namely, that in the Holy Supper only bread and wine are present, distributed, and received orally. Others, however, are subtle Sacramentarians, the most harmful kind, who in part talk our language very plausibly and claim to believe a true presence of the true, essential, and living body and blood of Christ in the Holy Supper but assert that this takes place spiritually by faith. But under this plausible terminology they really retain the former crass opinion that in the Holy Supper nothing but bread and wine are present and received with the mouth.

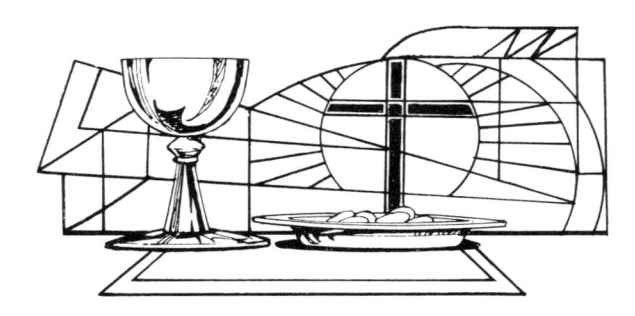

To them the word "spiritual" means no more than the presence of Christ's spirit, or the power of Christ's absent body, or His merit. They deny that the body of Christ is present in any manner or way, since in their opinion it is confined to the highest heaven above, whither we should ascend with the thoughts of our faith and there, but not in the bread and wine of the Holy Supper, seek the body and blood of Christ (Formula of Concord, Epitome, VII, 3–5).

FOR DISCUSSION

1. What was the basis for Zwingli's denial of the real presence in the Lord's Supper?
2. How did Zwingli and his group use Scripture to bolster their argument?
3. Why was Calvin's doctrine of predestination not Scriptural? What comfort do you get from the doctrine as explained by Luther?
4. What did Calvin mean by a "spiritual" presence of Christ in the Lord's Supper? How *is* Christ present?
5. How would you answer a friend who visited your church and criticized the artwork in the sanctuary because the Bible does not say we should have it? What kind of art work do you like in church? Why?
6. Summarize what the Bible teaches about the Lord's Supper.

A WORD FROM THE WORD

How good and pleasant it is when brothers live together in unity! . . . For there the Lord bestows His blessing, even life forevermore.

Psalm 133:1, 3

SESSION 18

The Reformation Spreads

... a time to build.
Ecclesiastes 3:3

You probably recall how St. Paul compared the church with a building: "**Each one should be careful how he builds. For no one can lay any foundation other than the one already laid, which is Jesus Christ**" **(1 Corinthians 3:10–11).** He goes on to say that fire will test the quality of one's work and refers to "hay or straw," which will be burned up, while "gold, silver, and costly stones" will survive.

The church in Luther's day needed that. They still confessed the Trinity, the deity of Christ, and the reality of sin, Satan, heaven, and hell. But the hay and straw of superstition and work-righteousness had all but covered the truths of God's Word. Now the Gospel came as a fire to burn up those parts of the building that were human notions and practices. It was a time to build by removing and replacing layers of falsehood that had accumulated over the centuries.

THE GOSPEL MOVES NORTH

Within 13 years, from 1527 to 1540, the Lutheran Reformation spread through all of Scandinavia (now Denmark, Norway, Sweden, and Finland), a remarkable feat without modern means of communication and transportation. A controversial king, Christian II (king of Denmark and Norway 1513–23, of Sweden 1520–23), who seemed to favor the pope one moment and Lutherans the next, put 80 Swedish leaders to death four days after his coronation in Sweden. But in Denmark he sided with the supporters of the Reformation against the Catholic clergy. While trying to make a Danish state church that he would control, he was driven into exile by the opposition.

Hans Tausen (1494–1561), a scholar who had heard Luther at Wittenberg, really deserves the credit for bringing Lutheranism to Denmark. Under Christian III (king of Denmark and Norway 1534–59) Lutheranism became the official religion of Denmark and Norway. Olavus Petri (ca. 1493–1552) and his brother Laurentius (1499–1573) brought the Reformation to Sweden, from where it spread to Finland.

... AND WEST

During the same years, the Swiss Reformation spread into France, Scotland, and the Netherlands (now Holland and Belgium). At least one fourth of the French population and half of the Netherlanders embraced Calvinism. John Knox (ca. 1513–72) of Scotland, after a rather checkered career which included time spent in Geneva, returned to his native country to begin a spirited campaign against the Romanists. His preaching so stirred up the people that they ravaged monasteries and smashed images. The lives of priests were threatened if they dared to say Mass.

Meanwhile in England, despite the earlier influence of William of Ockham and John Wycliffe (see session 8), the Reformation came slowly, mostly because of the opposition of the crown. Henry VIII (king of England 1509–47) took issue with Luther's *Babylonian Captivity of the Church;* for this he was named "Defender of the Faith" by the pope. It became popular to burn Luther's writings, but his teachings continued to spread.

A peculiar set of circumstances turned Henry against Rome, and the Reformation took root. In 1503 Julius II (pope 1503–13) gave the king permission to marry Catherine of Aragon, daughter of Ferdinand and Isabella of Spain and widow of Henry's deceased brother. They had six children, but only one daughter survived. Henry wanted to divorce Catherine because he believed that she would not give him a son, and no woman had ever ruled England.

Through Cardinal Wolsey, who had his own ambitions, Henry appealed to Clement VII (pope 1523–34) to annul the marriage. He did not, however, tell the pope that he had fallen in love with Anne Boleyn. But recent political victories of Charles V (see session 13), a nephew of Catherine, persuaded the pope to deny the divorce.

Prime Minister Thomas Cromwell urged Henry to separate the English church from Rome, become the head of the newly liberated church, and get the divorce. A series of acts by the parliament validated the break with Rome, and Henry married Anne Boleyn after Thomas Cranmer, archbishop of Canterbury, declared the divorce from Catherine to be official. When the king was excommunicated by the pope in 1534, Henry had the parliament pass the Act of Supremacy, which stated that Henry and future kings shall be the only supreme head of the Church of England.

In 1536 Cranmer drafted the Ten Articles as the confession of the Church of England. He based them on the Augsburg Confession, for he was greatly influenced by Luther. Bible translations, including the Great Bible, were made and published, and Henry mandated congregations to buy copies. He asked the priests to urge their people to read them.

In time, however, Henry reversed his position again and directed the parliament to pass several articles: Mass is to be continued, the Communion cup is to be denied to the laity, priests are not to marry, private Mass is efficacious, and confession is to be enforced. But during the reign of his son, Edward VI (king 1547–53), these articles were repealed and Protestantism came back to stay. Cranmer developed the *Book of Common Prayer,* as it was later called, and the Forty-two Articles, later reduced to the Thirty-nine Articles, which became the confession of the Church of England for centuries.

ROME RETALIATES

In 1540 the newly organized Society of Jesus (called the Jesuit Order) received papal approval. It was begun by Ignatius Loyola (1491–1556), a Spanish nobleman who was wounded in battle. Troubled by his sins, he entered a Dominican monastery, where he came to the conclusion that the way to find God's peace was by total subjection to the church. The Jesuits vowed complete obedience to the pope. They regarded Protestant doctrines, those that had surfaced in the Reformation, as the work of the devil; they had to be destroyed. If necessary, this would have to be accomplished by unethical means: "The end justifies the means" (or, if the cause is right, wrong can be committed to attain the goal).

The Jesuits emphasized education. They started a number of preparatory schools (separate from or in connection with universities). They developed a strong devotion to church authority. Jesuit priests delivered sermons that promoted practical Christianity, avoiding dogma and attacks on Protestantism. They revived Catechetical instruction; people were taught the fundamentals of the faith. The Jesuits differed from the other orders; they did not wear habits and were excused from certain monastic duties. The strong Jesuit educational program and propaganda did much to halt the spread of the Reformation.

The Holy Office was established in 1542 to stamp out heresy by means of trying and convicting offenders. Secular governments carried out the punishments (which could be death or imprisonment), and the popes, in turn, supported the Inquisition.

A final effort to stem the Protestant tide and to regain lost territory was the Council of Trent, held from 1545 to 1563. In three meetings the council defined church doctrine, made sweeping reforms, declared Protestant teachings (such as justification by faith) to be heretical, and confirmed the dogma that the pope alone had the right to interpret canons and decrees. However, not until the Vatican Council of 1870 was papal infallibility clearly defined.

The Catholic Counter Reformation lasted 150 years. During this time Catholic and Protestant armies often battled each other. As a result, Protestantism was almost completely snuffed out in Poland and southern Europe, but under Gustavus Adolphus and his Swedish army the Protestants were victors in northern Europe.

FOR DISCUSSION

1. What roles did Christian II and Christian III play in the spread of Lutheranism in Scandinavia? What was the role of politics in those events?
2. How successful was the Swiss reformation in western Europe? What would happen in your city if a reformation met with such success?
3. Why did Henry VIII turn against Rome?
4. Give examples from Scripture of times when God brought good out of evil. Does this still happen today? Explain.
5. Describe the three means of retaliation that were used against Protestantism.
6. Under what conditions might you be tempted to say, "The end justifies the means"? How does that argument stack up against Scripture?

A WORD FROM THE WORD

You will arise and have compassion on Zion, for it is time to show favor to her; the appointed time has come. For her stones are dear to Your servants; her very dust moves them to pity. The nations will fear the name of the Lord, all the kings of the earth will revere Your glory. For the Lord will rebuild Zion and appear in His glory.

Psalm 102:13–16

SESSION 19

The Formula of Concord

... a time to heal.

Ecclesiastes 3:3

Luther's last major task was to settle a dispute between two brothers. Once this was done, he became seriously ill, first complaining about a sharp chest pain. After several such attacks, he commended himself to God. In the end he was asked, "Reverend Father, are you willing to die in the name of Christ and the doctrine you have preached?" He answered "yes" clearly and loudly. He died on Feb. 18, 1546.

PEACE AT ANY PRICE?

Luther's death spared him from seeing his followers become sharply divided during the 30 years that followed. His dear and close friend, Melanchthon, was pressured to give in on certain church practices called *adiaphora* (ah-dee-AH-for-ah, "matters of indifference")—in this case ceremonies that are neither commanded nor forbidden in Scripture.

The Lutherans were pressed to surrender their position against the authority of the pope, confirmation by bishops, extreme unction, fasting regulations, and the Corpus Christi procession. Melanchthon and others were willing to make some concessions. Perhaps under some circumstances much of the above would have been tolerated, but this was a time of *confession,* not *compromise.* One of the chapters in the Formula of Concord (Article X: Church Usages) deals conclusively with the issue:

We believe, teach, and confess that at a time of confession, as when enemies of the Word of God desire to suppress the pure doctrine of the holy Gospel, the entire community of God, yes, every individual Christian, and especially the ministers of the Word as the leaders of the community of God, are obligated to confess openly, not only by words but also through their deeds and actions, the true doctrine and all that pertains to it, according to the Word of God. In such a case we should not yield to adversaries even in matters of indifference, nor should we tolerate the imposition of such ceremonies on us by adversaries in order to undermine the genuine worship of God and to introduce and confirm their idolatry by force or chicanery. It is written, "For freedom Christ has set us free; stand fast therefore, and do not submit again to a yoke of slavery," Gal. 5:1.

GOOD WORKS: NECESSARY? DETRIMENTAL?

The second controversy has been called "Majoristic" because it came into being through the teaching of Georg Major, a devoted disciple of Melanchthon. Even before this, Luther had warned against using the misleading statement that good works are necessary for salvation. Scripturally speaking, good works always follow justifying faith—they are necessary fruits that result from faith, but they have no place in justification itself.

Because the issue was of such great importance, another friend of Luther, Nikolaus von Amsdorf, went so far as to say that good works were injurious to salvation. (In fact, Scripture teaches that they are harmful if we put our trust in them.) Article IV (Good Works) of the Formula of Concord settles the matter:

We correctly reject the propositions that good works are necessary for the believers' salvation, or that it is impossible to be saved without good works, since such propositions are directly contrary to the doctrine of exclusive terms in the articles of justification and salvation (that is, they are diametrically opposed to St. Paul's words which exclude our works and merit completely from the articles of justification and salvation and ascribe everything solely to the grace of God and the merit of Christ . . .) . . . .

Concerning the proposition that good works are supposed to be detrimental to salvation, we give the following clear answer: If anyone draws good works into the article of justification and rests his righteousness or his assurance of salvation on good works in order to merit the grace of God and to be saved thereby, it is not we, but Paul himself, who declares no less than three times in Phil. 3:7 ff. that good works not only are useless and an impediment to such a person but are actually harmful. The fault, however, lies not with the good works themselves, but with the false confidence which, contrary to the express Word of God, is being placed upon good works. But it does not follow herefrom that one may say without any qualifications that good works are detrimental to believers as far as their salvation is concerned. For when good works are done on account of right causes and for right ends, . . . they are an indication of salvation in believers (Phil. 1:28).*

JUST A LITTLE BIT ON OUR PART?

"You can accept Christ," preaches the revivalist. "Do it today! Do it now!"

Perhaps no teaching surfaces more frequently than the notion that we somehow cooperate in our salvation (a teaching called synergism—"working together"). Melanchthon wavered on this point, too. A partner of his, Johann Pfeffinger, maintained that one has the free will to "decide for Christ," as we hear it said today. Article II of the Formula of Concord (Free Will) emphatically states:

Holy Scriptures ascribe conversion, faith in Christ, regeneration, renewal, and everything that belongs to its real beginning and completion in no way to the human powers of the natural free will, be it entirely or one-half or the least and tiniest part, but altogether and alone to the divine operation and the Holy Spirit. (Formula of Concord, Solid Declaration, II, 25.)

DO WE STILL NEED THE LAW?

People also twisted God's Word when they taught that the person who has been struck down by the Law and has come to faith in Christ no longer needs the Law. Johann Agricola, who had been rebuked by both Luther and Melanchthon, argued for this view. Article VI of the Formula of Concord (Third Use of the Law) disposed of the Antinomian Controversy (*anti:* "against"; *nomos:* "law"):

The law of God serves (1) not only to maintain external discipline and decency against dissolute and disobedient people, (2) and to bring people to a knowledge of their sin through the law, (3) but those who have been born anew through the Holy Spirit, who have been converted to the Lord and from whom the veil of Moses has been taken away, learn from the law to live and walk in the law. . . .

Although true believers are indeed motivated by the Holy Spirit and hence according to the inner man do the will of God from a free spirit, nevertheless the Holy Spirit uses the written law on them to instruct them, and thereby even true believers learn to serve God not according to their own notions but according to his written law and Word, which is a certain rule and norm for achieving a godly life and behavior in accord with God's eternal and immutable will.

Eight other articles of faith, mostly doctrines we touched on during previous sessions, were also included in the Formula of Concord. It was first signed by six theologians on May 29, 1577. Over 8,000 more pastors, teachers, etc. signed during the next three years. The document brought peace and healing throughout the Lutheran church.

FOR DISCUSSION

1. What was the danger in retaining certain ceremonies neither forbidden nor commanded in God's Word?
2. In what sense can we use the word *necessary* when we speak about good works?
3. How would you answer the question, "If we have the power to reject Christ, why don't we have the power to accept Him?"
4. Why is it incorrect to argue that true believers no longer need the Law?
5. The Bible clearly teaches that our salvation is *completely* God's work. How does that truth affect the way you feel, act, and speak?

A WORD FROM THE WORD

Your word, O Lord, is eternal; it stands firm in the heavens. Your faithfulness continues through all generations; You established the earth, and it endures. Your laws endure to this day, for all things serve You.

Psalm 119:89–91

SESSION 20

Concluding Activities for Unit 2

TERMS AND PEOPLE

Write brief definitions of the terms and brief descriptions of the people that follow:
1. The righteousness of God
2. Priesthood of believers
3. Indulgences
4. Confutation
5. Anabaptists
6. Mennonites
7. Libertines
8. Sacramentarians
9. Predestination
10. Jesuits
11. Holy Office
12. Adiaphora

SHORT ANSWER

Write a short answer to each of the following questions:
1. What event strongly influenced Luther's decision to enter the monastery?
2. Who was Johann Tetzel?
3. Why was Luther disappointed when he visited Rome?
4. Describe Luther's translation of the New Testament into German. Why did he do it?
5. How did the followers of Muenzer differ from the Mennonites?
6. What do you consider one of the most significant aspects of Luther's family life?
7. Contrast Luther's view of the Lord's Supper with that of Zwingli.
8. What attributes of God did Calvin emphasize?
9. Where in Europe did Lutheranism spread from Germany?
10. Why did Henry VIII of England break with the Roman church?
11. In what way does the teaching of synergism disagree with God's Word?
12. What is the "Third Use of the Law"?

UNIT 3
Christianity after the Reformation

"I just don't understand John. He hardly ever misses church, and he always seems very willing to lead devotions at our youth league meetings. But the language he uses at other times is something else! And you should see him at those Friday night parties!"

Do you know anyone like John? His life-style shows two kinds of contradictory behavior—a contradictory life-style, something as old as the Pharisees!

After the Reformation and on into the 20th century, movements in the church show how religion may sound orthodox (that is, the right doctrines are held), but the orthodoxy just covers up unchristian behavior. Other movements rose in reaction, movements that preached "deeds, not creeds."

Of course, those who insist on pure doctrine respond that, if your creeds aren't right, neither will your deeds be right.

In spite of this tension, the good news of salvation in Jesus Christ spread during these centuries; history shows a renewed interest in evangelism and worldwide missions.

SESSION 21
Pietism

Do two walk together unless they have agreed to do so?

Amos 3:3

ORTHODOXY

"Orthodoxy" means to have the right doctrine or teaching. As we learned in previous sessions, Luther and his followers worked hard to define and defend pure doctrine. We surely do not fault them for that. But events in the years that followed were not healthy.

The Thirty Years' War ended in 1648, leaving in its wake unbelievable devastation. One-third of the population of Germany had been killed or had died from disease and starvation. In one province in south Germany 8 towns, 45 villages, and 30,000 buildings had been leveled. Food at times became so scarce that dead bodies with grass in their mouths were found, and there was evidence of cannibalism. The war also caused a dehumanizing of the people.

In spite of the Reformation emphasis on the priesthood of all believers, there was much class distinction—a great gap between the upper and lower classes of society. At the church the upper class insisted on receiving Communion from a cup different from that given to the lower classes. They refused to have their infants baptized in water that had been used to baptize children of the lower classes.

The pastors tended to side with the more well-to-do instead of giving consolation to their entire flock. Many of them would preach against the Catholics, Calvinists, and Anabaptists, Sunday after Sunday. The Bible became an arsenal against those "stupid dogs" and blasphemers. When these pastors did preach the Gospel (namely, what God did for us) they said little or nothing about how this should bring about His work in us.

PIETISM

Precisely at this point pietism took issue with such kinds of "orthodoxy." Right doctrine was fine, but it must result in right living. Pietests taught that true religion had more to do with the heart than with the head. Johann Arndt, son of a Lutheran pastor, boldly asserted that purity of doctrine cannot be preserved without a holy life; true piety must include both faith and the fruit of faith.

Pietism was not an organized movement, nor did its adherents agree how the Christian life should be carried out. Men like Philipp Jacob Spener (1635–1705) promoted Bible classes for the laity, active participation in church work, the elimination of all references to false teaching and false teachers in sermons, and a lesser use of creeds. He condemned the theater, dancing, and cardplaying and taught moderation in eating, drinking, and dress. The Puritans who came to America had an affinity with the pietistic movement.

August Hermann Francke (1663–1727), Spener's close friend, held the same views, but tried to put the concepts of pietism into practice by creating institutions for orphans, the elderly, criminals, and unwed mothers. At one time the institution at Halle had 2,200 students and 300 teachers and workers. Francke expressed great concern over the training of pastors, believing that seminaries should stress pious living, not cold, abstract doctrines. The professors should take students along on pastoral calls to show them how to deal with parishioners and organize religious devotions in the home.

While neither Spener nor Francke wanted to form a new church, they encouraged the formation of groups within the congregation that would set examples of pious living to other members of the parish. These groups, called "cells" (made up of "true believers"), created resentment on the part of those who chose not to be part of the "inner circle." Instead of serving as leaven, they caused divisiveness and strife in the Lutheran church.

Pietism (which included a greater emphasis on the final coming of Christ than on the sacraments) was an understandable reaction to "orthodoxy." However, it lacked the freedom and joy that should attend the Christian life. An atmosphere of legalism and gloom pervaded pietism.

THE MORAVIANS

Another expression of pietism developed through the work of Count Ludwig von Zinzendorf, who was

Spener's godson. He obtained an estate near Dresden and opened it up to refugees in 1722, naming it "Herrnhut" (the Lord's Watch). Various denominations were represented: Lutheran, Catholic, Reformed, Brethren.

The colony was not intended to be a separate church. Rather, each denominational group was thought of as a temporary station before all would unite into one. Residents were asked to attend services at the local Lutheran church, but they themselves were organized as a congregation in the colony. It was headed by 12 elders and met for daily worship. Foot washing, the kiss of fellowship, and the love feast were introduced as Biblical and pious practices. Other practices of this group included separate houses for single men and single women, marriages if and when the church approved them, sunrise Easter services, a weekly "hour of song," Bible texts chosen by lot as daily "watchwords," and the sending of missionaries all over the world.

A definite connection exists between the Moravians who settled in England and the beginning of Methodism. Peter Boehler, a Moravian, had couseled John Wesley as the latter searched for peace with God. After Wesley's "experience" (session 22), he visited Herrnhut and later adopted some practices he observed, such as the love feast and the class meeting.

Like Spener, Zinzendorf was indifferent about formulas of doctrine. This caused him to be banished from Saxony in 1736. Undaunted, he visited the West Indies and America. In his absence, the Herrnhut community became an independent church called the "Unity of the Brethren." The name "Moravian" was often used, because many of the members originally came from the province of Moravia in Czechoslovakia.

FOR DISCUSSION

1. How does war affect the religious beliefs of people? Speculate on how the Thirty Years' War provoked friction.
2. Why does orthodoxy appeal to some people? Why does it fail to meet needs for others?
3. In what way is the expression "dead orthodoxy" a contradiction in itself?
4. Discuss Spener's teachings. Consider good and bad aspects.
5. What brought about tensions in congregations where pietism was introduced? What can a congregation today do to prevent similar tensions from arising?
6. Which do you regard to be more important: professing true doctrines or leading a Christian life? Give reasons for your choice.

A WORD FROM THE WORD

If an enemy were insulting me, I could endure it; if a foe were raising himself against me, I could hide from him. But it is you, a man like myself, my companion, my close friend, with whom I once enjoyed sweet fellowship as we walked with the throng at the house of God.

Psalm 55:12–14

SESSION 22

Methodism, Rationalism, and Deism

I despise your religious feasts; I cannot stand your assemblies.

Amos 5:21

"What known sin have you committed since our last meeting?"

"What temptations have you met with?"

"How were you delivered?"

"What have you thought, said or done, of which you doubt whether it be a sin or not?"

"Have you nothing you desire to keep secret?"

These are the five regular questions that the followers of John Wesley (1703–91) were asked at the 12-member society meetings ("bands" or "classes") he organized in England. Such probing was designed to lead to confession and accountability—which would foster a holier life. The band leader might also ask each person, "Do you desire to be told all your faults? Do you desire that, in doing this, we should come as close as possible, that we should cut to the quick, and search your heart to the bottom?"

JOHN WESLEY AND METHODISM

Like Martin Luther and Philipp Jacob Spener, John Wesley (an ordained clergyman in the Church of England) had no intention of founding a new denomination. However, as a result of his ministry, the Methodist church was organized and became the third-largest church body in America.

In the 1730s John and his brother Charles became known as extremely pious students at Oxford University. They gathered together a group of like-minded young men and formed what others derisively called the "Holy Club," where their studies included the Greek New Testament and Christian classics. They also participated in regular fastings, Communions, and prayers. They were not tract-pushers, and certainly not hypocrites, but honest and decent men who wanted to improve their personal Christian lives.

In October 1735, the Society for Promoting Christian Knowledge sent John and Charles to Georgia to do mission work. On shipboard, John was up every morning at four and back to bed at nine in the evening. Three fourths of the waking hours he spent praying, reading the Bible, learning the German language, preaching, and conversing with other passengers about one's relationship with God.

John kept a journal in which he wrote about a Moravian pastor on board who asked him if the Spirit of God bore witness with his spirit that he was a child of God. Wesley wrote that he was silent. He was then asked if he "knew" Jesus Christ. He responded by saying that Christ was the Savior of the world. "But has He saved *you?*" the pastor asked.

Wesley answered, "I hope so."

"But do you know yourself?"

John said that he did, but there was no conviction behind his answer. Three storms threatened the safety of those aboard, and he wrote that he was terribly frightened, not prepared to die.

Three years after his arrival in Georgia, John was back on board a ship headed for England, a man frustrated and filled with self-hatred over his failure as a missionary. Once home again he met with Peter Boehler of the Moravians, wanting to find out why he had not found God's peace. Had he not spent innumerable hours in prayer? Had he not fasted and communed again and again?

Deeply troubled, he attended a Moravian meeting at Aldersgate Street on May 24, 1738. Luther's *Preface to Romans* was read that night. In his journal Wesley wrote: "About a quarter before nine, while he was describing the change which God works in the heart through faith in Christ, I felt my heart strangely warmed. I felt I did trust in Christ, Christ alone, for salvation; and an assurance was given that He had taken away my sins, even mine, and saved me from the law of sin and death."

George Whitefield (1714–70) and John's brother Charles (1707–88) had similar experiences, and shortly thereafter the Methodist movement was born. For 50 years John traveled throughout England, preaching several times a day, writing, and organizing the bands, or societies. Charles wrote thousands of hymns and, like Lutheranism, Methodism was "sung" into the hearts of the people. Whitefield became the greatest orator of the three, attracting as many as 20,000 persons at an outdoor meeting.

Methodism became a separate church body after John's death in 1791, mostly because of the refusal of the Church of England to recognize clergy who were not ordained by Anglican bishops. (Apostolic succession had become one of the "signs of the true church" in England already in 1559.)

Prominent in Methodism were a genuine *conversion* to Christ and *perfectionism*. The disciplines Wesley enjoined on his preachers illustrate this, as he wrote in his *Large Minutes:*

"We might consider those that are with us as our pupils; into whose behavior and studies we should enquire every day. Should we not frequently ask each other, 'Do you walk closely with God? Have you now fellowship with the Father and the Son? At what hour do you rise? Do you punctually observe the morning and evening hour of retirement? Do you spend the day in the manner which we advise? Do you converse seriously, usefully, and closely?' To be more particular, 'Do you use all the means of grace yourself, and enforce the use of them on all other persons?' "

For the ministers, he wrote: "Do you ask everywhere, 'Have you family prayer?' Do you retire at five o'clock? How do you fast every Friday? Christian conference: Are you convinced how important and how difficult it is to 'order your conversation right'? Do you converse too long at a time? Is not an hour commonly enough?"

For common Christians and preachers: "Do you never miss your class, the Band? Do you deny yourself every useless pleasure of sense, imagination, honour? Are you temperate in all things? Do you eat no flesh suppers? Do you eat no more at each meal than is necessary? Are you not heavy or drowsy after dinner? Do you drink water? Why not? Did you ever? Why did you leave it off? If not for health, when will you begin again? Today? How often do you drink wine or ale? Every day? Do you want it?

"Wherein do you 'take up your cross' daily? Do you cheerfully bear your cross (whatever is grievous to nature) as a gift of God, and labour to profit thereby? Do you endeavor to set God always before you; to see His eye continually fixed upon you? Never can you use these means but a blessing will ensue. And the more you use them the more you will grow in grace."

(Wesley quotes above are taken from *The Works of John Wesley* [Grand Rapids: Baker Book House, 1979].)

RATIONALISM AND DEISM

Methodism was in part a reaction to the cold, formal practice of religion in the state church of England.

Another movement of that time was influenced by the revolutionary scientific discoveries of men like Copernicus, Galileo, and Newton. This movement—rationalism—stressed the importance of basing professed truths on known facts. Rationalists revived discussion about human dignity, free will, religious liberty and our alleged ability to do God's will.

Human reason (Latin: *ratio*) became the authority. This resulted in deism, which acknowledged the existence of God, but did not recognize the Trinity or God's activities in human affairs. Deists revived the old heresy of acquiring bliss after death by virtuous living. Many of the American Founding Fathers, including a number of early Presidents, were deists.

FOR DISCUSSION

1. Do you think John Wesley had saving faith before the Aldersgate Street experience? Why or why not?
2. Put yourself into John Wesley's shoes on a boat to America. Have you *known* Jesus Christ? Has He saved *you?* (Do not write your answer unless you wish. Think deeply about the question. Then be ready to talk about it during class.)
3. What contributions did Charles Wesley and George Whitefield make to the Methodist movement?
4. Why did the Methodists become a separate church body?
5. If you were asked to join a group who would ask members the questions Wesley wrote for his followers, how would you respond? Why?
6. What was the greatest weakness of the Methodist movement?

A WORD FROM THE WORD

My soul faints with longing for Your salvation, but I have put my hope in Your word. . . . Your word is a lamp to my feet and a light for my path.
Psalm 119:81, 105

SESSION 23

Christians Come to America

I sent rain on one town, but withheld it from another.
Amos 4:7

Luther once said that the Gospel is like a summer rain: It doesn't stay in one place, but soon passes on to another land. Today in Denmark, where the Reformation first took root after its beginnings in Germany, only 4 percent of the people attend church at least once a month. Only 1 percent of those between the ages of 25 and 34 go to church once a month. Twenty-five per cent of the people believe that Christ is the Son of God, and only 30 percent believe in a life after death.

In this session we will take a look at Christianity as it moved westward. Already by 1500 America was regarded as a field "white for harvest." Both native Americans and Europeans, the latter having emigrated to North America and often abandoning their connection with the church, were prime targets.

CONQUESTS BY SPAIN

When Columbus returned after his famous discovery, King Ferdinand II of Spain asked Alexander VI (pope 1492–1503) to ratify his ownership of the new territory. In 1494 the pope established a line of demarcation that ran north and south, declaring that land east of it would be Portugal's and land west of it belonged to Spain. Under this arrangement, Brazil became the possession of Portugal, and everything west of it went to Spain. Even today Brazilians speak Portuguese, while people in the rest of South America use Spanish.

Hernando Cortés led much of the conquest of Central America. At the age of 31 he led an expedition of 500 men into Mexico. Montezuma, king of the Aztecs, and Mexico City fell into his hands in 1519/21.

Another activist was Fray Marcos de Niza, a Franciscan friar, who traveled on foot from Mexico City to upper Arizona and New Mexico, assuring the American Indians that they would not become slaves of the *conquistadores*. But already the white man's lust, greed, and brutality in the Caribbean Islands was becoming known. Back home, the Roman church mandated that the conquests be carried out in harmony with Christian principles, but to little avail. The conquered natives perceived that the Christian "god" was gold.

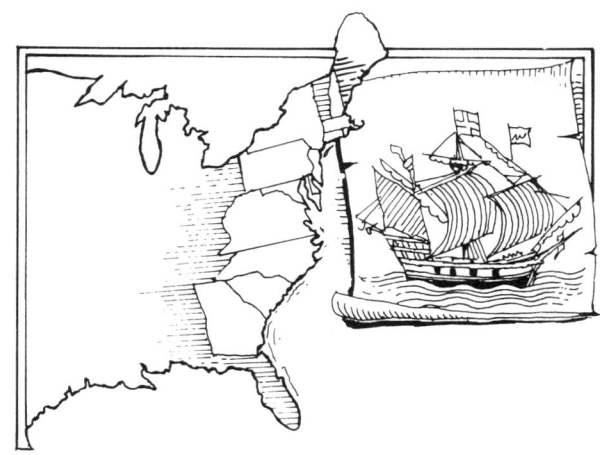

The Franciscans worked among the Indians in New Mexico, Arizona, and California. Santa Fe (Holy Faith), founded ca. 1609, became their headquarters. One hundred thousand were converted to the Catholic faith by the middle of the 17th century. Meanwhile, French explorers, often accompanied by Jesuits, traveled the rivers and the Great Lakes of North America, founding Quebec in 1608.

EARLY ENGLISH EFFORTS

Only after the defeat of the Spanish Armada did England take up the task of converting the American Indians in the New World. James I (king of Great Britain 1603–25) fostered two expeditions, claiming ownership of the northeast American coast 100 miles out to sea and 100 miles inland.

Early settlers, especially in Jamestown, VA, were beset with rotten food, rats, famine, and sickness. During the winter of 1609–10 the population dwindled from 490 to 60. But the following year a capable preacher, Alexander Whitaker, "Apostle of Virginia," spearheaded a movement to convert the natives. The Jamestown effort marked the start of the Episcopalian church in America.

In 1620 a group called Separatists (who believed the Church of England was corrupt) settled at Plymouth, Massachusetts. William Bradford was their leader. Congregations, not bishops, had ruling authority. Still others (led by John Winthrop) settled in the

Massachusetts Bay Colony in 1630; they tried to establish a pure church (Puritans).

Some years later the infamous "Witches of Salem" trials were held. In the spring of 1692 a number of young girls were accused of witchcraft. Some 20 were executed in Salem before sanity was restored by Judge Samuel Sewall, a member of the local court.

BAPTIST BEGINNINGS

Roger Williams (ca. 1603–83), an Anglican clergyman, came to Salem in 1631. There he collided with civil authorities by stating that the native Americans, not the English crown, were the rightful owners of the land. He also proclaimed the importance of keeping church and state separate and soon was banished from Massachusetts. He then organized a colony in Providence, Rhode Island, and founded a Baptist church in 1639. While the early Baptists in America were divided (the General Baptists held that a person's eternal election depended on his or her acceptance of Christ; Particular Baptists believed in a doctrine of predestination similar to Calvin's), the movement grew to become the largest Protestant denomination in America.

QUAKERS AND MENNONITES

George Fox (1624–91) spent 40 years as a traveling preacher in England, proclaiming the necessity of "inner" illumination in order to understand the Bible properly. His open defiance of civil authority and of forms of Christianity other than his own caused such a disturbance that he was jailed for a time.

Fox and his followers organized the Society of Friends, who were derisively called Quakers. The title came about when one of The Friends warned a judge that he would quake on Judgment Day. The judge replied, "No, thou shalt be the quaker." Carrying the priesthood of all believers to an extreme, they had no ministers and regarded the sacraments as unnecessary. They were known especially for their meetings, during which all sat in silence until "the Spirit" caused someone to speak. After being banished from Massachusetts and Virginia, they settled in New Jersey, Delaware, and Pennsylvania.

The Mennonites agreed with the Quakers in their refusal to bear arms. Many German Mennonites settled at Germantown, now a part of Philadelphia, where some became Quakers.

LUTHERANS LAND

The first Lutherans in America were Swedes who settled at Fort Christina (now Wilmington), Delaware, in 1638 and built three churches. Johan Campanius (1601–83), a Swedish pastor, translated Luther's Small Catechism into the language of the Delaware Indians, the first Protestant book published in an Indian tongue. The colony eventually became Anglican.

German Lutherans settled in 1734 near Savannah, Georgia, having fled from persecution in Salzburg, Austria. They organized in 10 congregations, but the Revolutionary War caused the colony to dwindle. Lutherans fared well, however, in Pennsylvania, where Henry Melchior Muehlenberg earned the title of Patriarch of the Lutheran Church in America. He brought order out of chaos by writing constitutions for congregations, a service book, and a hymnal during the 1740s.

Not until 1838/39 did the fathers of the future Lutheran Church—Missouri Synod leave Saxony and settle in and around St. Louis. While Martin Stephan (1777–1846) brought the group to these shores, the leadership soon went to C. F. W. Walther (1811–87), who organized the synod that would become known for its strong doctrinal position, worldwide missions, and educational system. While refusing altar and pulpit fellowship with other church bodies until agreement in doctrine and practice was established, Walther worked hard among American Lutherans to bring about unity based on God's Word and the Lutheran Confessions, as we will hear in session 32.

FOR DISCUSSION

1. Discuss the tension between Christian missionary efforts in the Western Hemisphere in the 17th century and the efforts of European powers to claim land and conquer native American nations.
2. Discuss how Christianity adapted itself and was adapted to the new world in the 17th century.
3. Consider "denominationalism" in light of "where you got off the boat."
4. To what extent did the American situation form religion in America?
5. What did Christians in Europe leave—and come to—when going to America?
6. Having now reviewed several other denominations, what are some teachings of Lutheran doctrine that you really appreciate?

A WORD FROM THE WORD

There is no speech or language where their voice is not heard. Their voice goes out into all the earth, their words to the ends of the world.

Psalm 19:4

SESSION 24

Religious Revivals in Early America

When a trumpet sounds in a city, do not the people tremble?

Amos 3:6

"CHRISTIAN" AMERICA?

Much of American history can be understood if we listen to the speech made by John Winthrop on the *Mayflower* even before he set foot on the shores of the New World.

Wee are entered into covenant with Him for this worke. . . . Now if the Lord shall please to hear us, and bring us in peace to the place wee desire, then hathe He ratified this covenant . . . but if wee shall neglect the observation of these Articles . . . and . . . shall fall to embrace this present world and prosecute our carnal intentions seeking great things for ourselves and our posterity, the Lord will surely break out in wrath against us, be revenged of such a perjured people and make us knowe the price of the breach of such a covenant.

Winthrop was saying that if we do God's will, He will bless; if not, He will punish. He meant this not just for the individuals, but for all the colonists as a group, and ultimately for the entire emerging nation. Probably most people held this notion, at least in theory, but only 10 percent held church membership.

New England Calvinism grew and bore fruit, yielding the colonial work ethic, rugged individualism, and institutions of higher learning such as Harvard and Yale. Benjamin Franklin coined the proverb, "God helps those who help themselves," a true reflection of "the Protestant work ethic," as it has been called, though Franklin himself was not a professing Christian.

FIRST REVIVAL

Arminianism, a European religious movement led by Jacobus Arminius (1560–1609) in the late 1500s, was thoroughly suppressed, but it surfaced in America a century and a half later. Arminians believed that humans are not totally depraved, and could, therefore, cooperate in their salvation; election to eternal life was conditional and not absolute; and Christ died for all, not just the elect. All this was contrary to Calvinism.

In order to interest the vast company of the unchurched, outdoor camp meetings were held, and thousands joined churches in New England, Virginia, and Kentucky. The focus was not so much on what God had done but on the way we respond to Him. Emotional sermons challenged sinners to repent and, because it was said that we have a free will, to choose salvation in Jesus Christ.

Two major figures, George Whitefield of England (whom we learned about in session 22) and Jonathan Edwards (1703–58), led the Great Awakening (ca. 1725–50), as this revival was called. Whitefield was a powerful preacher, so dramatic and convincing that at one point he attracted a single audience of 30,000 in Boston. Because of the appeal to emotions, the sermons would often bring about laughter, screaming, convulsions, crying, and alleged visions both at and after camp meetings.

The hearers were not just the lower, uneducated class. Even Benjamin Franklin, patriot and deist, was moved by Whitefield's oratory. In his autobiography of 1739 Franklin wrote that he had had no intention to give any money when the collection was taken after Whitefield's sermon. But as he listened, he began to soften. First he decided to give a handful of copper coins; later, his pocketed silver money; and in the end he included everything, even his "five pistoles of gold."

Whitefield made six visits to the States, bluntly stating in his sermons that congregations were "dead" because "dead men" preached to them.

Edwards tried to retain Calvinism, but his sermons did imply that we are able to accept forgiveness. In general the Great Awakening stressed "individual decision," the "necessity of the Christian to be able to identify the day and the hour" of his conversion, and the need for every Christian to win an unbeliever for Christ.

SECOND REVIVAL

Charles G. Finney (1792–1875), who claimed a personal conversion in 1821, was a major figure in a second general revival (ca. 1800–1830). Trained as a lawyer, he used methods that evoked dramatic responses from his hearers. He would shout actual names of persons in the congregation and invite them to the "anxious bench" down front where, after much verbal turmoil, they would be persuaded to grasp personal salvation in their decision to accept Christ.

This virtually buried the tenets of Calvinism, which limited salvation to the elect; now anyone could be saved, and everyone had to bear the responsibility of where he or she would spend eternity. In his *Lectures on Revivals of Religions* (1835), Finney defended his rather bold techniques of arousing the sinner:

If we examine the history of the church we shall find that there never has been an extensive reformation, except by new measures. Whenever the churches get settled down into a "form" of doing things, they soon get to rely upon the outward doing of it, and so retain the form of religion while they lose the substance. And then it has always been found impossible to arouse them so as to bring about a reformation of the evils, and produce a revival of religion, by simply pursuing the established form. . . . When (God) has found that a certain mode has lost its influence by having become a form, He brings us some new measures which will BREAK IN upon their lazy habits, and WAKE UP a slumbering church.

Earlier Protestant hymns had emphasized the awful majesty of God and the magnitude of His grace, but with the new stress on humanity's response, "Gospel hymns" (which appealed to emotion) became popular. This was especially evident in the ministry of Dwight L. Moody (1837–99), the most notable evangelist during the late 1800s. His partner was Ira D. Sankey (1840–1908), a hymn writer and singer who would accompany himself on a reed organ, leading Gospel songs with conviction and emotion. A sample of Moody's sermons will illustrate his style (taken from *Moody's Great Sermons,* 1899):

Now, let me say, my friends, if you want that love of God in your hearts, all you have to do is to open the door and let it shine in. It will shine in as the sun shines in a dark room. Let Him have full possession of your hearts. Some people have an idea they had something to do to bring about reconciliation. God is already reconciled. There is not anything for you to do but believe that God is reconciled.

But all was not directed to the hereafter. Moody maintained that success here below would surely follow true conversion, but that, on the other hand, unless the heart is made right with God, "all else will be wrong." Persons saved by the blood of Christ do not become subjects of charity, but rise to respectable heights and comforts. Success is bound to follow for those who put Christ first in their lives.

This "theology of success" is exactly what is being propounded by many preachers in the "electronic church" of today.

The sacrifices of Methodist circuit riders and Baptist farmer-ministers contributed much to the success of the revivals as the movement headed west. Especially the lower middle class welcomed the Baptist worker-ministers who, quite on their own, organized local families into congregations. By the mid-1800s the U. S. had 1,500,000 Methodists (then the largest Protestant denomination) and 1,000,000 Baptists.

FOR DISCUSSION

1. Define "revival." What images come to mind when you think about a revival meeting? Does the term have a positive or negative connotation for you? Why?
2. "Revival" implies a bringing back to life. Do you ever feel your spiritual life needs to be "revived"? Explain.
3. Discuss what it means to be spiritually "high"; to be spiritually "dead."
4. What are some dangers to your spiritual life if you get into the habit of needing to be "revived"?
5. Discuss the power of a "great" preacher you have heard. What does he do to you? How do you feel an hour later? 48 hours later?
6. List the great evangelists of today.
7. Does America need a revival today? Why or why not?

A WORD FROM THE WORD

When I kept silent, my bones wasted away through my groaning all day long. For day and night Your hand was heavy upon me; my strength was sapped as in the heat of summer. Then I acknowledged my sin to You and did not cover up my iniquity. I said, "I will confess my transgressions to the Lord"— and You forgave the guilt of my sin.

Psalm 32:3–5

SESSION 25

19th-Century Mission Activities

Let justice roll on like a river, righteousness like a never-failing stream!

Amos 5:24

At times the church has been accused of being preoccupied with internal matters—pure doctrine, pure living, proper organization, etc. Some say that we have forgotten our main purpose, to bring the saving Gospel to all people: **"Go and make disciples of all nations" (Matthew 28:19).**

LUTHERAN PREOCCUPATION?

The Preface to the *Book of Concord* lists five reasons why Lutherans gathered these doctrinal statements in 1580. The first two are "to the increase and expansion of God's praise and glory" and "to the propagation of that Word of his that alone brings salvation." Both reflect a mission-mindedness. The early Lutheran church was not preoccupied only with holding to the pure doctrine.

Of course, the early Lutheran efforts to bring the Gospel into heathen lands faced enormous barriers like control of the sea lanes by hostile powers, as well as poor transportation, unknown languages, unfavorable climate, and tropical diseases. Activities like "The Lutheran Hour" and "This Is the Life" came much later.

Mission societies sprang up throughout Europe at the beginning of the 1700s. The Halle-Danish mission was founded in 1705; the same year it sent missionaries Bartholomaeus Ziegenbalg and Heinrich Pluetschau to India. By the end of the century some 60 missionaries were sent from Halle. Hans Egede went from Denmark to work with the Eskimos in Greenland from 1722 to 1736. His son Paul succeeded him there, translating the New Testament into the language of the people. A hundred years after the beginning of the Halle mission, the Berlin Missionary Society renewed the effort.

BIBLE SOCIETIES

It became immediately evident that if these new churches would thrive at all, someone would have to translate the Bible (or at least parts of it). The Canstein Bible Institute in Germany led the way in 1710, but it took nearly another hundred years before the British and Foreign Bible Society (1804) and Bible societies in America took up the task.

By 1906 the British and French Bible Society had close to 6,000 branches in the United Kingdom. A year later the society reported that 204,000,000 Bibles, testaments, and portions of Scripture had been circulated.

The American Bible Society had a goal not only to place a Bible in every home in the land, but to produce translations for foreign fields. By the mid-1960s it had translated the Bible into 1,280 languages and dialects.

WILLIAM CAREY

The first major British and American foreign mission thrusts were directed to India and then to China. More than any other person, William Carey (1761–1834), a short, humble cobbler, gave impetus to the movement in the 1800s. While Carey was in India, a Hindu carpenter named Kristno dislocated his arm and came to the Baptist Missionary Society for help. A member of the group reduced the swelling.

Kristno was so impressed that he ate with the missionaries in public, a practice forbidden in his caste. An angry crowd hauled him before the Danish governor of the district who, to their surprise, commended rather than punished him. William Carey took Kristno to the banks of the River Hooghly and delivered a sermon that condemned the notion that the river had magical powers. He then baptized this first Hindu convert in the river by immersion. In time, Carey learned the languages of India well enough to translate the whole Bible into Bengali and parts of it into numerous other languages and dialects.

ADONIRAM JUDSON

Some early missionaries endured immense hardship as they witnessed for Christ. One such person was Adoniram Judson (1788–1850), an American who proclaimed the Gospel in Burma. When a war broke out between Great Britain and Burma in 1824, he was arrested as an enemy alien and imprisoned for 17 months.

Judson's wife did what she could to get food and medicine to him and pleaded with the royal family for his release. In a letter to her brother-in-law, she related his plight: Judson and the other white foreigners were confined in prison, each wearing three pairs of iron fetters that were fastened to a long pole. Judson was moved to three prisons, always followed by his faithful wife and children, but was finally released.

The efforts of Judson moved other Protestants to join in the missionary activities in the Far East.

DAVID LIVINGSTONE

No single person was more responsible for calling the attention of the world to the African slave trade than David Livingstone (1813–73), who arrived in South Africa in 1841, to do mission work. Before his journey he visited the wards of London hospitals to learn what he could about medicine. In the beginning he attempted to open new mission stations in the "dark interior" of the continent. Later he devoted his energies to combating the slave traders and to exploration. It was his conviction that the way to end the profitable slave trading was to open trade routes from the coasts so that Africa could develop commercially. His work in exploration eventually led to worldwide recognition.

For 30 years Livingstone traveled all over the continent, seeking the support of native chiefs. During these years he fought warring tribes, struggled with malaria, and was bitten by a lion. The American public saw him as a romantic adventurer undertaking a good cause. In 1871 a reporter, Henry Stanley, was sent by the *New York Herald* to find him. In 1871 they met, and Stanley's question about identity became famous: "Dr. Livingstone, I presume?"

HENRY OPUKAHAIA

In the early 1800s, missionaries from America came to Hawaii at the urging of Henry Opukahaia, who had been trained to become a pagan priest in Hawaii, where he was born. As a teenager he saw his parents killed in a tribal war, jumped from a rocky cliff into the sea, and swam to an American ship anchored in Kealakekua Bay. He begged the captain to take him to America where, after arriving, he was given a home with a professor at Yale (New Haven, Connecticut). There he visited churches, pleading with the people to send Christian missionaries to his homeland.

Liholiho (Kamehameha II, king of Hawaii 1819–24) met with the missionaries of the American Board of Commissioners for Foreign Missions on April 14, 1820, not at all convinced that this new religion was a good thing. Grinning at his five wives, he told the white men that if he accepted their ways he would have to give up four of his wives. They did win him over and he became quite a force for Christianity in Hawaii.

By 1832 Hawaii had 900 schools with 54,000 students. Eighty percent of the people could read and write by the mid-1800s, a truly remarkable feat. Unlike efforts in other lands, the cause was greatly aided by the support of royalty.

FOR DISCUSSION

1. Demonstrate that the Lutheran church has shown, and continues to show, an interest in mission activities.
2. Do we have a choice in deciding whether or not to carry out mission activities? Explain your answer.
3. Describe obstacles that had to be overcome by the early missionaries to foreign countries.
4. What obstacles do you face as you contemplate mission activities? How can these obstacles be overcome?
5. Do you consider David Livingstone to be a hero? Why or why not?
6. Missionaries believe that God has called them to give their lives to this work. If you were inclined to become a full-time missionary, what steps would you take to become certain of the calling? In what missionary activities can you participate *now,* without leaving your family and friends?

A WORD FROM THE WORD

May God be gracious to us and bless us and make His face shine upon us; may Your ways be known on earth, Your salvation among all nations. May the peoples praise You, O God; may all the peoples praise You. May the nations be glad and sing for joy, for You rule the peoples justly and guide the nations of the earth.

Psalm 67:1–4

SESSION 26
The Church and Social Issues

Hate evil, love good, maintain justice.
Amos 5:15

Should the church speak out on social issues, especially those that are not clearly dealt with in Scripture? In recent decades churches have been asked to apply Scriptural principles to such issues as temperance (prohibition of liquor), labor, and slavery. In 1987, for example, the Roman Catholic Church took a stand against test-tube fertilization, artificial insemination, and surrogate motherhood. All churches continue to wrestle with problems brought on by the legalization of abortion and by the teaching of evolution. Like it or not, churches are involved in social issues today.

THE SOCIAL GOSPEL

Men like Adolf von Harnack and Walter Rauschenbusch fostered the idea of the Social Gospel. They saw Jesus as Liberator, not as Redeemer. When Christ spoke of the kingdom of God, they claimed, He did not mean the church (the believers), but a transformed and renewed society. This came to be known as the Social Gospel.

In session 44 you will contrast Social Gospel with "social ministry." While the Social Gospel sees Jesus as Liberator instead of Redeemer, social ministry flows out of God's love as shown to us in the redeeming work of Jesus. Those who accept this love by faith respond with love for their fellow human beings and minister compassionately to all their human needs—spiritual, physical, emotional, social, and economic.

Perhaps no other single contribution to the cause of social ministry was more effective than Charles M. Sheldon's novel, *In His Steps,* which had sales of 30 million, second only to the Bible in the publication of books. In the opening chapter a tramp interrupts a worship service and asks, "What do you Christians mean by following the steps of Jesus?" Sheldon then describes activities of people who pledged not to do anything for a year without first asking the question, "What would Jesus do?"

TEMPERANCE

Attention was drawn to the evils of alcohol in the early 19th century, when the liquor business was flourishing as never before. At times religious revivals ignited campaigns against the sale of intoxicating drinks. John Gough, a former bookbinder with some experience on stage, began to make appearances in pulpits and theaters in America and Great Britain with the goal of obtaining "temperance pledges." Millions (according to estimates) came to watch him dramatize the tragic life of a drunken father and husband, but considerably fewer actually "took the pledge" to deny themselves any further use of liquor.

In 1826 the American Society for the Promotion of Temperance came into being. Laws passed during the 1850s forbade the production and sale of liquor, except for medicinal purposes, in 13 states. Later the Women's Christian Temperance Union was formed, followed by the Anti-Saloon League of America in 1895. Colorful figures like Carrie Nation actually led raids on saloons, but the WCTU generally favored political action and gave its support to the National Prohibition Party (formed 1869). By the early 1900s, 19 states prohibited liquor sales, and in 1919 a constitutional amendment made prohibition a law of the land (until 1933, when this amendment was repealed).

LABOR

The rights of the common laborer and the abolition of child labor were championed especially by the Methodists, who adopted a "social creed" in 1908. This later became the platform of the Federal Council of the Churches of Christ in America. It advocated

—Christian practices in obtaining and using wealth and the lessening of the profit motive;

—living wages and proper shares for all workers;

—safe working conditions;

—insurance in cases of accidents, old age, unemployment, and sickness;

—a shorter working week and shorter working day;

—better environment for women workers;

—abolition of child labor;

—fair prices for farm products, taking into consideration overhead;

—protection against intoxicants;

—fair treatment of lawbreakers (courts, jails);

—equal rights for all racial, religious, and economic groups;
—reduction of armaments and rejection of war as a solution to resolve international disputes;
—construction of a world order for peace;
—freedom of the press and toleration of open assemblies; and
—free speech.

SLAVERY

More than any doctrinal disagreement, the issue of slavery split major Protestant denominations in the United States. The American Antislavery Society, organized in 1833, met open and sometimes violent opposition. A notable incident occurred in Alton, IL, where Elijah P. Lovejoy was killed by a mob that also destroyed his printing press.

A plan offered to prevent bloodshed and end slavery was circulated by the American Colonization Society of 1817. Essentially it meant the return of blacks to Liberia (Africa). Leaders of major denominations were behind it, but little materialized.

In the North the seminaries strongly favored the abolition of slavery, maintaining that it was contrary to God's Word. (See **Philemon 15–16** and **Matthew 23:8**.) Many Southern church leaders disagreed. They argued that the Biblical account of Noah and his sons **(Genesis 9:22)**, which they interpreted as meaning that Ham (signifying "burnt" or "black" according to the old commentators) was punished and became the father of the Negro peoples, proved that slavery was in accord with Scripture.

Slavery occasioned splits in the Methodist, Presbyterian, and Baptist churches. The Methodist Episcopal Church, South, and the Southern Baptist Convention came into existence in 1845.

SOAP, SOUP, AND SALVATION

Known for its military uniforms and bands, the Salvation Army, founded by William Booth in 1865, brought ridicule from the traditional churches, but turned out to be a force that reached the masses. Booth aimed to convert the souls of society's outcasts by showing that their bodies were also precious in God's sight. While the use of military titles and terminology offended leaders in the churches, the program appealed to the hungry and defeated. No new doctrines were added, only an emphasis on what was derisively called "soap, soup, and salvation."

FOR DISCUSSION

1. How did the Social Gospel differ from the Gospel proclaimed in the New Testament epistles?
2. How does the Gospel of Christ (for example, **John 3:16**) motivate you to perform social ministry? List some areas of social ministry in which students in your school can make a difference.
3. Consider pledging for *one day* (or even one hour) not to do anything without first asking the question, "What would Jesus do?" Then talk about the experience. How did it change your behavior? Would you like to live that way for your entire life? Would you like others to live that way? Why or why not? Where did you get the strength to act like Jesus? What did you do when you failed to keep your pledge?
4. How can we deal with the problems of alcoholism? What effect on alcoholism does the passing of laws that prohibit the manufacture and sale of liquor have?
5. With which positions in the "social creed" of the Federal Council of Churches do you agree? With which ones do you disagree?
6. Show that the "Noah-Ham" account does not support slavery. What guidelines do you follow in your relationships with other people?
7. In what way does the Salvation Army meet needs that have been largely neglected by most churches? What is your congregation doing (if anything) to meet similar needs?

A WORD FROM THE WORD

Do not let the oppressed retreat in disgrace; may the poor and needy praise Your name.
Psalm 74:21

SESSION 27
19th-Century Threats to Christianity

I will send a famine . . . of hearing the words of the Lord.

Amos 8:11

Every year on the first Sunday in Lent the account of the three temptations of Jesus by the devil is read in many churches. Dostoyevsky, a great Russian writer, said that if the record of these temptations had been lost, all the combined wisdom of the world could never replace it. Each one is aimed at a basic human need, each contains an element of truth, and each suggests a shortcut to the desired goal.

While revivalism, foreign missions, and the Social Gospel flourished during the 1800s, three extreme views that affect us today emerged in Europe. Each contains a flavor of the three temptations, and their departure from the authority of Scripture truly ushered in a **"famine of hearing the words of the Lord" (Amos 8:11)**.

"TELL THESE STONES TO BECOME BREAD"

The Communists disdain to conceal their views and aims. They openly declare that their ends can be attained only by the forcible overthrow of all existing conditions. Let the ruling classes tremble at a communist revolution. The proletarians have nothing to lose but their chains. They have a world to win. Working men of all countries, unite!

So wrote Karl Marx (1818–83) and Friedrich Engels (1820–95) in the *Communist Manifesto* of 1848. Marx had attended German universities and aspired to become a professor, but his radical views of reforming society kept him from carrying out his ambition. He became a journalist and was eventually expelled from Germany. In London he teamed up with a like-minded revolutionary, Friedrich Engels, in stirring up agitation and publishing materials calling for radical reform in society.

Marx was angry about the inequalities of the classes; to him, the comfort of the ruling upper-middle class could not be reconciled with the miserable lot of the majority, who were impoverished laborers in the mines and factories and on farms. He denounced the church and rejected the notion of a God who guided human history.

Marx held that reality was "matter," not spirit and not nature. History, therefore, was determined by the way people related to material things. The greatest good was happiness for all here and now, not in some hoped-for life to come, and this could be brought about by material prosperity.

The lower classes had as much right to that prosperity as the "capitalists." Consequently, they must change society by force until all class distinctions are eliminated. Then the state would take over, and private property would cease to exist. The slogan "Religion is the opiate of the people" was coined because Christianity especially called for obedience to the constituted authority.

"THEY WILL LIFT YOU UP IN THEIR HANDS"

Friedrich Schleiermacher (1768–1834) was the son of an army chaplain who stressed pietism. Friedrich himself favored neither pietism nor orthodoxy. He developed a concept of religion based on "experience," which led to "dependence." All Christian doctrines were

59

to be interpreted in this light. "God," then, is that on which we feel dependent. "Sin" is our failure to feel dependent. Christ (who was not God, but was human) is the best example of a person being totally dependent on "God." His mission was to teach others about this complete dependence.

Schleiermacher did not believe that religion was a set of doctrines to be accepted. Nor was Christianity the only valid religion, though it was superior to others. The feeling of dependence, he held, is common in all religions that share the desired goal of bringing men into harmony with God. The Bible was not, as the Lutheran Confessions taught, the Word of God, but rather a record of the experiences of people who "had the Word of God." All who are dominated by the "consciousness of God" make up the church. While the world is hostile to the church, Schleiermacher held out the hope that in the end the world would be changed and everyone would be saved.

Making "experience" the norm (in place of the written Word) opened the door to all manner of deviations—not only from distinctive Lutheran teachings, but from the basic doctrines in the creeds. This subjective approach to Scripture led to the "liberal" notion that the Bible could be researched like any other historical writing in order to determine the validity of its contents.

The denial of miracle accounts followed. Jesus was seen as an ideal example of morals and self-sacrifice, but not as the sin-atoning God-Man revealed in Scripture. The authorship of Biblical books was questioned: Moses did not write the first five books of the Bible, which were woven together by an editor who used several other sources. This "higher critical" methodology will be taken up in future sessions.

"IF YOU WILL BOW DOWN AND WORSHIP ME"

We're amazed at Satan's arrogance when he asked Jesus to worship him. But great arrogance was also shown at the Roman Catholic Vatican Council in 1870. This council declared that the pope is infallible when he speaks on questions of faith and morals *ex cathedra* ("from [his] chair"—"officially"), a claim that has never been withdrawn. Pius IX (pope 1846–78) occupied the papal throne at the time.

Two other important issues occurred under Pius IX. The first of these was the papal proclamation that the Virgin Mary was from the time of her conception "immune from all taint of original sin." Four years after the 1854 proclamation, a peasant girl (Bernadette Soubirous) said that Mary had appeared to her in a grotto near Lourdes, France, no less than 18 times. On the Feast of the Annunciation the girl claimed Mary told her, "I am the immaculate conception." During the next half-century it was reported that some five million persons came to Lourdes seeking a miraculous cure.

A second issue was the Syllabus of Errors (1864). It condemned 80 "errors" condemned by Pius IX. Some of these were

1. all truths of religion stem from human reason;
2. miracles in the Bible are fictional;
3. the church must not judge philosophy;
4. one can find eternal life in any religion;
5. Protestantism is another form of the Christian religion;
6. ecclesiastical courts should be abolished;
7. public schools should have no church authority governing them;
8. church and state should be separated;
9. divorce may be pronounced by civil authority;
10. a civil marriage is proper for Christians;
11. the state has jurisdiction over marriages.

FOR DISCUSSION

1. Why do you think Karl Marx developed such a large following?
2. Which are the most serious problems with Communism as espoused by Marx?
3. As Schleiermacher viewed it, what was the guiding principle in the interpretation of Scripture? What is a proper guiding principle?
4. Because of a subjective view of Scripture, what traditional understandings of the Bible were rejected by many scholars? How can we respond to those who hold such a view?
5. Respond to the three issues that arose during the papacy of Pius IX.
6. With which "errors" in the pope's Syllabus do you agree? With which ones do you disagree?

A WORD FROM THE WORD

Rescue me, O Lord, from evil men; protect me from men of violence, who devise evil plans in their hearts and stir up war every day. . . . O Lord, I say to You, "You are my God." Hear, O Lord, my cry for mercy. . . . Surely the righteous will praise Your name and the upright will live before You.

Psalm 140:1–2, 6, 13

SESSION 28

Fundamentalists Battle Evolutionism

He will pull down your strongholds and plunder your fortresses.

Amos 3:11

On July 21, 1925, the headlines of the Louisville, Ky., *Courier Journal* read: "3,000 at Trial, Get Thrill!"

Place: Dayton, Tenn.

Purpose: To determine whether or not John T. Scopes, a public-school teacher in Tennessee, was guilty of violating a state law by teaching evolution.

In attendance: 100 newspaper reporters; lemonade vendors (the heat was unbearable); a huckster who set up a booth, complete with monkey; Clarence Darrow, an agnostic (one who claims he can't know if there is a God) who would defend Scopes; William Jennings Bryan, who had lost the race for the presidency of the United States three times, as the prosecutor; 12 mostly uneducated farmers, who would make up the jury; Judge T. Raulston, the presiding official; and hundreds of Fundamentalists.

WHO WERE THE FUNDAMENTALISTS?

In the last session we noted the beginnings of liberalism, which tried to do away with the supernatural in Christianity. Reaction set in. Leaders in several Protestant denominations in America supported the publication of 12 books entitled *The Fundamentals* between 1909 and 1915. Five doctrines were defended as being the absolute minimum needed to support Biblical Christianity. They were

—the inspiration and infallibility of Scripture;
—the deity of Christ (including His virgin birth);
—the substitutionary atonement of Christ's death;
—the literal resurrection of Christ from the dead;
—the literal return of Christ in the Final Advent (Coming).

The theory of evolution, of course, was contrary to a Bible that was authored by God and that clearly taught creationism.

THE EVOLUTION OF EVOLUTION

In 1859 Charles Darwin, an Englishman who had studied medicine and theology, published *On the Origin of Species by Means of Natural Selection*. In it he set forth the principle of the survival of the fittest, or natural selection. Plants and animals adjust and develop new capacities so they can cope with their surroundings. When the capacities become fixed, a new species evolves. All of life began with the simplest of forms, and the process has taken millions of years. "God" was unnecessary.

This evolutionary theory flatly contradicted the creation account in Genesis.

ON WITH THE TRIAL

Scopes was declared guilty of breaking the law and fined $100. But the trial became significant because Darrow, his attorney, made Bryan (the prosecutor and defender of creationism) look foolish. When cross-examined by Darrow, Bryan appeared trapped. The heart of the trial went like this:

Darrow: Mr. Bryan, do you believe that the first woman was Eve?

Bryan: Yes.

D: Do you believe she was literally made out of Adam's rib?

B: I do.

D: Did you ever discover where Cain got his wife?

B: No, sir; I leave the agnostics to hunt for her.

D: You have never found out?

B: I have never tried to find out.

D: The Bible says he got one, doesn't it? Were there other people on the earth at that time?

B: I cannot say.

D: You cannot say. Did that ever enter your consideration?

B: Never bothered me.

D: There were no others recorded, but Cain got a wife.

B: That is what the Bible says.

D: Where she came from you do not know. All right. Does the statement, "The morning and the evening were the first day," and "The morning and the evening were the second day," mean anything to you?

B: I do not think it necessarily means a 24-hour day.

D: You do not?

B: No.

D: What do you consider it to be?

B: I have not attempted to explain it. If you will take the second chapter—let me have the book. (Examines the Bible.) The fourth verse of the second chapter says: "These are the generations of the heavens and of the earth, when they were created in the day that the Lord God made the earth and the heavens." The word "day" there in the very next chapter is used to describe a period. I do not see that there is any necessity for construing the words, "the evening and the morning," as meaning necessarily a 24-hour day, "in the day when the Lord made the heaven and the earth."

D: Then, when the Bible said, for instance, "and God called the firmament heaven. And the evening and the morning were the second day," that does not necessarily mean 24 hours?

B: I do not think it necessarily does . . . .

D: You think those were not literal days?

B: I do not think they were 24-hour days.

D: What do you think about it?

B: That is my opinion—I do not know my opinion is better on that subject than those who think it does.

D: You do not think that?

B: No. But I think it would be just as easy for the kind of God we believe in to make the earth in six days or in six years or in 6,000,000 years or in 600,000,000 years. I do not think it important whether we believe one or the other.

D: Do you think those were literal days?

B: My impression is they were periods, but I would not attempt to argue as against anybody who wanted to believe in literal days.

D: Have you any idea of the length of the periods?

B: No, I don't.

D: Do you think the sun was made on the fourth day?

B: Yes.

D: And they had evening and morning without the sun?

B: I am simply saying it is a period.

D: They had evening and morning for four periods without sun?

B: I am simply saying it was a period.

D: They had evening and morning for four periods without the sun, do you think?

B: I believe in creation as there told, and if I am not able to explain it, I will accept it. Then you can explain it to suit yourself.

D: Mr. Bryan, what I want to know is, do you believe the sun was made on the fourth day?

B: I believe just as it says there.

D: Do you believe the sun was made on the fourth day?

B: Read it.

D: I am very sorry; you have read it so many times you would know, but I will read it again (reads **Genesis 1:14–19**). *"And God said, let there be lights . . . and the evening and the morning were the fourth day." Do you believe, whether it was a literal day or a period, the sun and moon were not made until the fourth day?*

B: I believe they were made in the order in which they were given there, and I think in the dispute with Gladstone and Huxley on that point—

D. Cannot you answer my question?

B: I prefer to agree with Gladstone.

D. I do not care about Gladstone.

B: Then prefer to agree with whomever you please.

D: Cannot you answer my question?

B: I have answered it. I believe that it was made on the fourth day, in the fourth day.

D: And they had evening and the morning before that for three days or three periods. All right, that settles it.

(Arthur Weinberg, ed., *Attorney for the Damned* (Chicago: Univ. of Chicago Press, 1989 [1957]). Copyright © 1957, 1989, by Arthur Weinberg. Reprinted with permission of Lila Weinberg.)

FOR DISCUSSION

1. Evaluate the five teachings that the Fundamentalists regarded as the minimum needed to support Biblical Christianity. What teachings would you add?
2. In what way did Darwin's theory of evolution contradict the Bible?
3. Describe Bryan's error in connection with a "day" of creation.
4. How would you have answered the question regarding Cain's wife?
5. How would you have answered the question regarding the existence of "evening and morning" before the creation of the sun and the moon?
6. Describe the impact of this trial since 1925.
7. Do you think public schools should teach the creationist theory? Defend your answer.

A WORD FROM THE WORD

By the word of the Lord were the heavens made, their starry host by the breath of His mouth. He gathers the waters of the sea into jars; He puts the deep into storehouses. Let all the earth fear the Lord; let all the people of the world revere Him. For He spoke, and it came to be; He commanded, and it stood firm.

Psalm 33:6–9

SESSION 29
Millennialism

Why do you long for the day of the Lord?
Amos 5:18

MILLENNIALISM

"Millennium" comes from the Latin *mille* ("thousand") and *annus* ("year"). The term "a thousand years" occurs in only one chapter of the Bible, **Revelation 20.** Largely on the basis of this chapter, some believe that there will be a visible kingdom of God on earth. *Premillennialism* is the view that Christ will come *before* the thousand years during which He will rule the earth. *Postmillennialism* has Christ coming after the thousand years.

Teachings about millennialism pose dangers to Christians. A document by the Lutheran Council in the USA, *What About the Millennium? A Statement to Lutherans,* identifies those dangers:

The manipulation of numbers and dates easily becomes a substitute for truly confronting the demands of the Word of God. Attention is thereby distracted from the true struggle of making moral choices, bravely facing the real enemies of God, and remaining faithful to His promises. . . .

A truly biblical apocalyptic vision opens up our relationships to include all others in God's world. Those who claim to provide a special insight into God's plan form an exclusive, elite, and often vengeful group set against the rest of humanity. Thus the very idea of a literal rapture which snatches the believer away from the world and death is a repudiation of the meaning of the cross and of Jesus' invitation to His followers to take up that cross and follow Him. We are asked to share in the sufferings of our Lord in and for the whole world. But the rapture becomes a personal hedge against the fear of suffering and death. To escape out of the world this way is a self-centered triumph contrary to the teaching of Jesus.

Millennialist thought tends to encourage a search for personal security by setting out a plan that unfolds in a predetermined way. In the midst of terror and chaos this predictable future provides assurance. But it also means that the believer is not really a participant in any of these events, because the plan works quite automatically. Against such conceptions stand the many parables and warnings in the New Testament calling us to watch actively for the coming of the Master (cf. Mark 13:34–37), who at the end will take account of our stewardship in the world.

A final objection to typical millennialist teachings is that the millennial hope is rarely linked in any significant way to the center of Christian hope, the resurrection of Jesus Christ. The resurrection of Jesus is the beginning of the future triumph of God and the vindication of His people. Our faith does not invite us to the security of knowing the calendars of the future nor to escape from the world. But it calls us into the world, to share its destiny in the light of the resurrection of Jesus.

(Used by permission of Division of Theological Studies, Lutheran Council in the USA).

DISPENSATIONAL PREMILLENNIALISM

The notion of a visible kingdom of Christ on earth is not a new idea. You may remember that the Augsburg Confession rejects the opinion of those who "teach that, before the resurrection of the dead, saints and godly men will possess a worldly kingdom and annihilate all the godless" (XVII 5). But a particular form of this view was originated by John N. Darby (1800–82), a founder of the Plymouth Brethren movement in England and Ireland during the 1800s.

The *Schofield Reference Bible* of 1909 gave Dispensationalism impetus on the American scene. Soon it became the most popular millennial belief. The largest Protestant body in America, the Southern Baptist Convention, approved it, as did the Campus Crusade for Christ and the Moral Majority. Television evangelists Pat Robertson and Jack Van Impe accept it, as does Hal Lindsey in his books. Briefly put, this is its scenario for the future:

1. An earthly kingdom involving Israel will be established by God.
2. Abraham's physical descendants will be given the land of Canaan.
3. The Messiah will rule over Israel in Jerusalem.

63

4. Old Testament promises will be fulfilled during the 1,000-year reign of Christ on earth.
5. God has two purposes: the earthly goals for the Jews and heavenly goals for true believers (the church).
6. The distinction between Jews and Gentiles will be revived and go on through eternity.

A "dispensation" is a period when people are tested in connection with their obedience to some particular revelation of God's will. There are seven such periods: Innocence **(Genesis 1–3),** Moral Responsibility **(Genesis 4–8),** Human Government **(Genesis 9–11),** Promise **(Genesis 12–Exodus 18),** the Law **(Exodus 19–Acts 1),** the Church **(Acts 2–Revelation 19),** and the Millennial Kingdom **(Revelation 20).** The following pattern is proposed:

Israel was promised an earthly kingdom to be ruled by the Messiah, Jesus Christ, who offered it to the Jews when He came. They rejected Him and the kingdom. So Christ initiated the "mystery form" of the kingdom, the church. This situation will end when believers will "meet the Lord in the air" (**1 Thessalonians 4:17,** called the "Rapture"), go to heaven with Christ, and celebrate the marriage feast for seven years.

According to **Revelation 6–19,** certain events will take place on earth during the seven years. The "tribulation" will commence, and will intensify during the later years, due to the reign of terror by the Antichrist. Judgments will fall on the earth, but a remnant of 144,000 will believe in Christ and preach the Gospel and the kingdom. Many will be saved, though wars will lead up to the battle of Armageddon.

Once the seven years are over, Christ and His own will return to earth, destroy His enemies, and convert most Israelites. Satan will be bound up for 1,000 years. The faithful who die during the tribulation will be raised and go to heaven. Living Gentiles will be judged; the "goats" will be thrown into hell and the "sheep" will begin the 1,000-year reign with their natural bodies. This will be a golden age of peace and prosperity, and worship will be centered in the rebuilt temple.

Some of the offspring, however, will not believe, but will join Satan for a final battle. Believers who die will be raised, and after Satan's "little season" the unbelieving dead will be raised and judged. Finally, the lasting distinction between Jew and Gentile will go into effect.

HISTORIC PREMILLENNIALISM

This differs from Dispensationalism in that:
1. Christ's return will happen after the tribulation, during which most Jews will be converted.
2. Both living and dead believers will meet Christ in the air and descend to earth, where Christ will kill the Antichrist, bind up Satan, and establish the 1,000-year earthly kingdom.
3. Christ and believers will rule over unbelieving nations. Sin and evil will still exist, but to a lesser extent.
4. After 1,000 years of peace and prosperity, Satan will be let loose for a final struggle with the believers, but will be defeated. Dead unbelievers will be raised for the final judgment of all people.

POSTMILLENNIALISM

Based on their interpretation of **Matthew 28:18–20,** postmillennialists believe that the whole world will become Christian. Evil will be the exception, and a golden age of peace and prosperity will exist until the end, when Christ returns.

SEVENTH-DAY ADVENTISM

The Seventh-day Adventists profess the following millennial concepts:

Christ entered the holy place of the heavenly temple on Good Friday and stayed there for 18 centuries to plead for sinners. In 1844 He went to the heavenly holy of holies, where He will remain until His return. Immediately before He returns, those who crucified Him and believing Adventists who died before 1846 will be raised in order to see His coming. He will then destroy the beast, the false prophet, and those who fought Christ and His people at Armageddon.

Satan will "bear" the sins of the world and live on a desolate earth for 1,000 years. All living and dead Adventists will enter heaven and, with Christ, will rule there 1,000 years. After that, the wicked will come to life and, together with Satan, attack the heavenly Jerusalem, which had come to earth. Satan, his angels, and the wicked will be annihilated. Christ and His believers will live eternally on a new earth.

FOR DISCUSSION

1. Summarize the dangers of millennialist teachings.
2. Which millennialist teachings (if any) do your acquaintances hold?
3. How can you witness to a millennialist?
4. Identify one error of each of the following:
   Dispensational premillennialism
   Historic premillennialism
   Postmillennialism
   Seventh-day Adventism
5. In your opinion, which of the above groups holding millennial views uses Scripture in the most arbitrary way? Defend your answer.
6. Read **Revelation 20.** What does this chapter say to you? How do you think the church should interpret this and other passages like it?

A WORD FROM THE WORD

Say among the nations, "The Lord reigns." The world is firmly established, it cannot be moved; He will judge the peoples with equity. . . . He comes to judge the earth. He will judge the world in righteousness and the peoples in His truth.

Psalm 96:10, 1:

SESSION 30
Concluding Activities for Unit 3

TERMS

Write brief descriptions of the terms that follow:
1. Pietism
2. Deism
3. Line of demarcation
4. Revivals
5. Bible societies
6. Social Gospel
7. Communist Manifesto
8. *Ex cathedra*
9. Fundamentalists
10. Liberals
11. Evolution
12. Millennium

SHORT ANSWERS

Write a short answer to each of the following questions:
1. What did the pietists have against orthodoxy?
2. What led to John Wesley's "conversion" experience?
3. Describe the faith of the early American settlers.
4. How does Arminianism differ from Calvinism?
5. What teaching of Dwight Moody is heard in the "electronic church" today?
6. Describe the early Protestant missionary efforts in India.
7. Why did missionaries succeed in Hawaii?
8. On what three concerns in American life did the Social Gospel touch?
9. How was the course of history determined, according to Karl Marx?
10. Why did William Jennings Bryan do so poorly at the Scopes trial?
11. Which millennial group divides the Bible into seven periods of history?
12. In what way does postmillennialism contradict the teachings of Christ? In what ways do all millennialists threaten to weaken the hope God has given us through Christ?

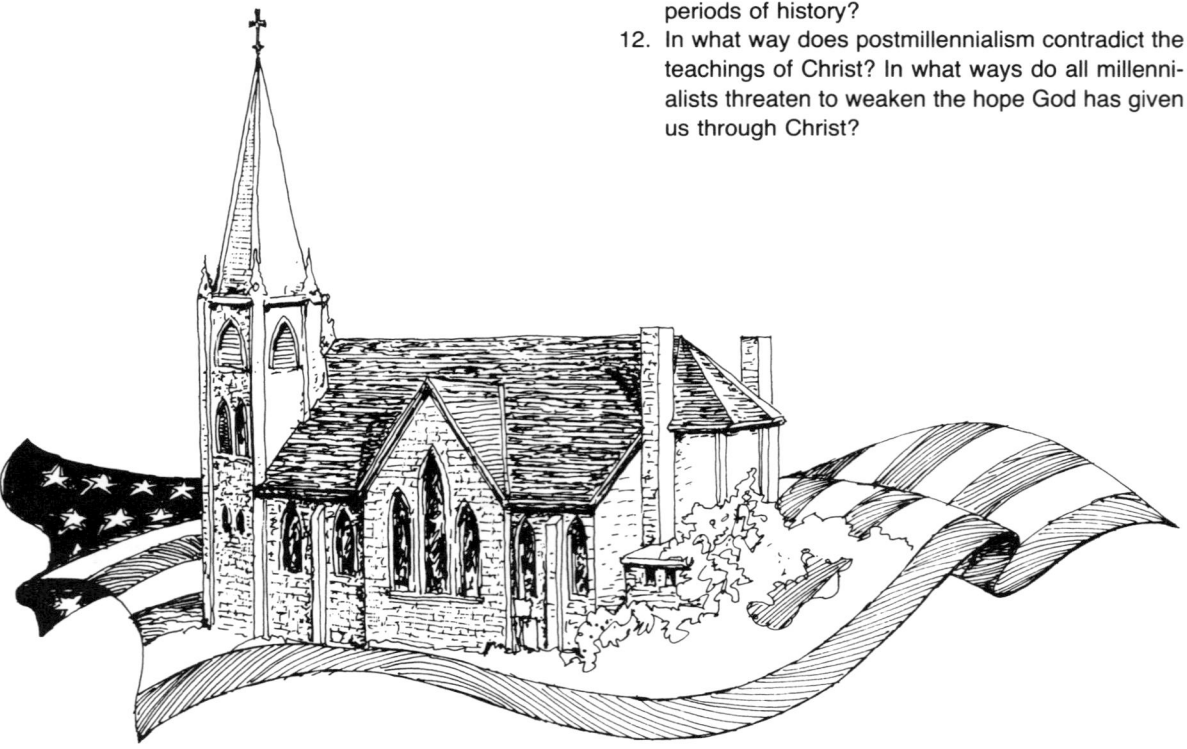

UNIT 4
Christianity in the 20th Century

The average American today moves 14 times during a lifetime. If you're average, you have already moved at least four times. When churchgoers relocate, they look for a new church home. Do they insist on transferring to a congregation of the denomination to which they belonged before they moved? Many don't. In fact, unless they have strong convictions, they may have joined five or more different denominations by the time they retire.

How can people become members of churches that have different beliefs? Many join out of convenience or because the people are friendly and exude love for one another. Pure doctrine and holy living simply don't rate that high in their decisions.

We have often studied about divisions, but the situation has changed. We live in an era of religious "coming-togetherness." Catholics and Protestants alike are seeking unity rather than searching for reasons to divide even more. As we study this recent phenomenon, we need to remember a word of caution: Christian unity is a great blessing *if the parties first agree on what they believe, confess, and teach.*

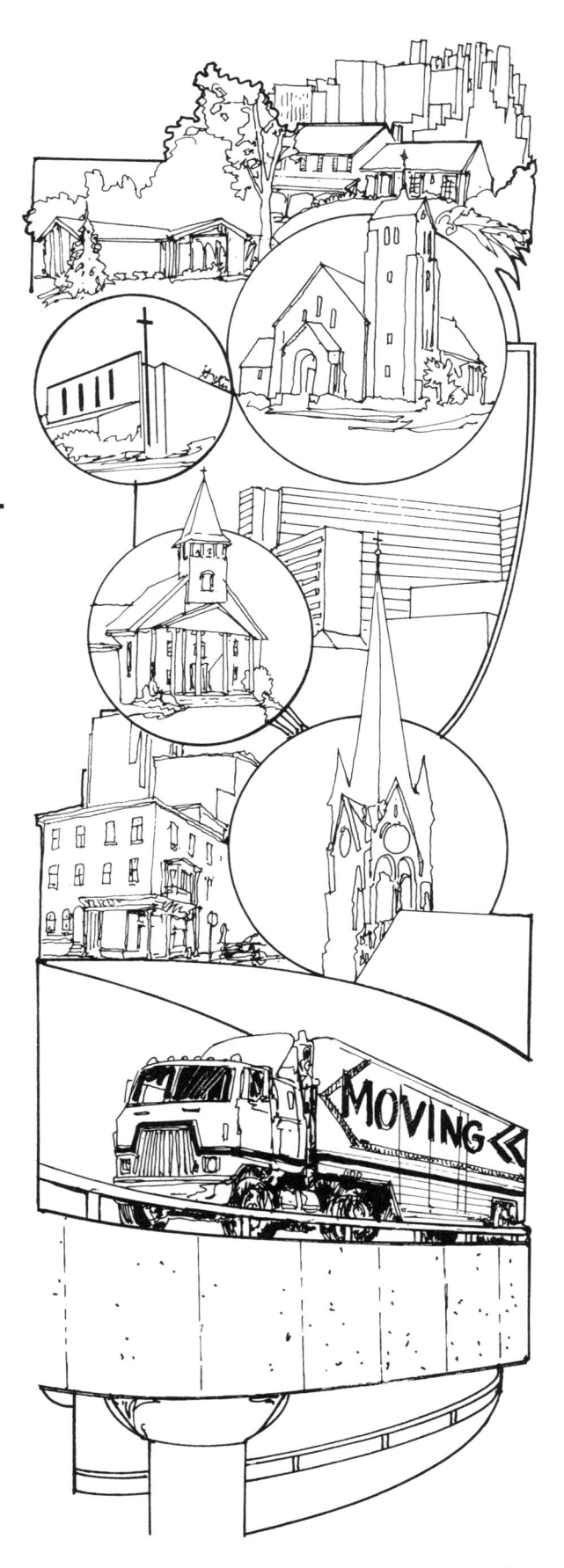

SESSION 31

Lutherans Come to America

"In that day," declares the Lord, "I will . . . assemble the exiles . . . ."
Micah 4:6

The early Lutheran immigrants from Europe often settled in rural and forest areas. Pastor F. C. D. Wyneken wrote of their situation:

Either singly or in small groups our brethren go into the forest with their wives and children. In many cases they have no neighbors for miles around, and even if they have such nearby, the dense forest so separates them that they live in ignorance of one another. . . .

Husband and wife and children must work hard to fell the giant trees, to clear the virgin forest, to plow, sow, and plant. Bread must be procured; but this can be gotten only from the ground which they till. . . .

Small wonder, then, that everybody works in order to support this body and life. No difference is made between Sunday and weekdays, especially since no church bell calls them to the house of God and no neighbor in his Sunday outfit arrives to call for his friend.

It is not to be wondered at that the pioneers' tired limbs seek their couch without prayer and that dire need drives them to leave it and return to work without prayer; even the prayer at mealtime has long since been banished by inveterate infidelity or recent trouble. Alas, Bible and hymnal also in many cases have been left in the Old Country, as the people, owing to rationalism, had lost taste for them. No preacher arrives to rouse them from their carnal thoughts and pursuits, and the sweet voice of the Gospel has not been heard for a long time.

(From W. G. Polack, *Fathers and Founders*. St. Louis: Concordia Publishing House, 1938, p. 47.)

THREE PROBLEMS

Wyneken's observations point out three of the problems of the early Lutheran settlers:
—lack of opportunity to assemble together;
—lack of time and energy for daily prayer and worship on Sunday; and
—a distaste for things religious (due to their recent encounter with rationalism).

Rationalists rejected the authority of events recorded in the Bible. Their approach to Scripture resulted in churches in Germany and elsewhere becoming lecture halls instead of sanctuaries. Sermons and hymns dealt with living a happier life here and now. They avoided references to sin, God's grace in Christ, and eternity. The sacraments became meaningless, and catechisms were devoid of anything uniquely Christian. The settlers wanted no part of what they had left behind, but what were they to do?

WHY THEY LEFT

In addition to rationalism, the Prussian Union caused many to leave Germany. In 1817 King Frederick William III proclaimed that Lutheran and Reformed churches in Potsdam (near Berlin) would hold a joint Communion service on October 31. Confessional Lutherans rejected this "forced" union of churches with opposite beliefs, but in the 1830s the Prussian government imprisoned pastors who wouldn't comply. Congregations were disbanded, and hundreds fled to America.

HELP IS ON THE WAY

Through Wyneken, Pastor Wilhelm Loehe of Neuendettelsau in Bavaria sent many missionaries to America to minister to the settlers. But he was also concerned about the spiritual needs of the American Indians, so he organized immigrant groups who went to the Saginaw Valley in Michigan. There the villages of Frankenmuth, Frankentrost, and Frankenlust (named after their forefathers, the Franks) were established. The Michigan District would become the largest segment in the forthcoming Missouri Synod.

ENTER THE SAXONS

Pastor Martin Stephan in Dresden did not approve of the Prussian Union. His simple but direct Law-Gospel sermons attracted many, but the public press denounced him as the founder of a radical new sect. He was attacked for holding private gatherings and for moral infractions. As a result, he was hauled into court. The charges were finally dropped, but he and his followers realized that the time had come to leave their homeland.

Before they set sail for New Orleans, on their way to St. Louis, Stephan published a farewell message that was carried in the Bremen newspapers. He thanked those who had come to the aid of those who had decided to leave—about 700 (including 6 pastors, 10 seminary students, and 4 teachers). Five ships left the port of Bremerhaven in the winter of 1838–39 but one of them, the *Amalia,* was lost at sea.

During the voyage Stephan convinced his followers to name him bishop, giving him authority in all spiritual and temporal matters. After arriving in St. Louis, he bought 4,500 acres of land in Perry County, about 100 miles south of the city. Some of the immigrants chose to remain in St. Louis. The colony was very disturbed when Stephan was accused of immorality and deported across the Mississippi to Illinois. His followers began to wonder if they should have left their homeland. Were they truly a church? Were the sacraments administered by their pastors valid?

C. F. W. WALTHER

The man who would come to their rescue and prevent the group from dividing was Pastor Carl Ferdinand Wilhelm Walther (1811– 87), a great theologian and teacher, one of the founders of the Missouri Synod. Like Wesley, he joined a circle of like-minded men (but at the University of Leipzig) who devoted themselves to prayer and the study of the Bible in order to offset the blatant rationalism being taught.

After Stephan was deposed, Walther engaged in a debate at Altenburg, Mo., in order to answer the nagging questions of the colonists. Walther convinced them that they were members of the true church—the total number of believers—and that they had the Word of God. When the Word of God is taught in its purity and the sacraments are administered according to Christ's institution among a visible group of confessing Christians, the church is present. Even those who had disagreed with this view before the debate were won over to Walther's views, and peace was restored.

FOR DISCUSSION

1. Compare the three problems confronted by the early Lutheran settlers with problems people face today.
2. Why did so many Germans leave their homeland? What would you do if you faced a similar situation?
3. Imagine that you have the task of telling relatives of those lost on the *Amalia* about the disaster. Write a telegram of 25 words or less to one of those relatives. Include a word of comfort.
4. According to Walther, where is the true church?
5. What constitutes a "church"? What do you need to have a church according to Scripture?
6. Related to the matter of forcing people to worship together, should parents insist that their children attend services? Explain your answer.
7. What evidence of God's grace do you find in the history recorded in this session?

A WORD FROM THE WORD

Let me understand the teaching of Your precepts; then I will meditate on Your wonders. My soul is weary with sorrow; strengthen me according to Your Word.

Psalm 119:27–28

SESSION 32

Growth of the Missouri Synod

You will be true to Jacob, and show mercy to Abraham, as You pledged on oath to our fathers in days long ago.

Micah 7:20

When a few congregations and pastors organized the Missouri Synod at Chicago in 1847, they were forming an organization that faced great possibility of failure.

WOULD IT GROW?

For one thing, the Synod began with only 12 congregations and 12 pastors (charter members), scattered over an area between Buffalo, NY, on the east and St. Charles County, MO, on the west. It included 4 congregations from Indiana, 2 from Ohio, 2 from Illinois, 2 from Missouri, 1 from Michigan, and 1 from New York. No railroads led to Chicago. Delegates came by way of the Mississippi and Illinois rivers, or by stagecoach, horseback, or buggy. Some had to travel on foot. Could a far-flung federation of congregations do a great deal together, much less grow?

A language problem also existed. The official name of the Synod was *Die Deutsche Evangelisch-Lutherische Synode von Missouri, Ohio und andern Staaten*. According to its constitution, its conventions had to use German exclusively. English was suspect because the revivalists used it, as did the Lutherans in the East, many of whom practiced fellowship with Reformed ministers and congregations. This, after all, was why the "Missourians" had left Germany. Outsiders viewed their refusal to commune with those who were not members of the Missouri Synod or to exchange pulpits with non-Lutheran preachers as hindrances to growth.

Yet, in 50 years the Synod numbered 687,334 members in 1,986 congregations and 683 preaching stations, with 1,564 pastors and professors. After 75 years there were over 3,000 pastors and over a million members. By 1985 over 8,000 pastors were on the roster, and 2,700,000 members belonged to over 6,000 congregations.

WHY THE GROWTH?

As St. Paul says, one person plants the seed, another waters, but God makes it grow **(1 Corinthians 3:6)**. But God uses human means and situations to build His church. One might point to the improved methods of communication and transportation that had developed since the birth of the Synod. The change from German to English in the early 1900s contributed. But the basic reason is reflected in Walther's words to Friedrich Brunn of Steeden, Germany (who sent over 200 men to serve as pastors): "Not our size, but rather our unity in doctrine, is our treasure." (From *Walther Speaks to the Church*, by Carl S. Meyer.)

Also, immediately at its first convention the infant denomination expressed concern about missions and education. That convention elected a committee to generate mission activities among the American Indians. They also took steps to educate pastors and teachers who would serve immigrants. The Missourians set a unique goal to establish an elementary (parochial) school in every congregation. A number of settlements had no public schools, and an education with a heavy emphasis on learning Scripture and Lutheran doctrine seemed vital to the future of the church.

SEMINARIES AND COLLEGES

Even before the organizational meeting in Chicago, seminaries had been established in Perry County, Mo., and Fort Wayne, Ind. In 1849 the Perry County seminary was moved to St. Louis. Walther served as its first professor, a position he held (along with a pastorate) until his death. Dr. Wilhelm Sihler served in a comparable position at the Fort Wayne seminary, which was later moved to St. Louis, then to Springfield, IL (where it stayed for many years), and more recently back to Fort Wayne.

Some of the Synod's greatest theologians taught at the seminaries. Franz Pieper, who served as a president of the Synod, wrote a three-volume *Christian Dogmatics*. It presented the teachings of the Lutheran Church in a detailed, systematic way.

To supply teachers for the schools of congregations, a private "teachers seminary" was opened at Milwaukee in 1855. It was transferred to Fort Wayne, then to Addison, IL, and then to River Forest, IL. A second teachers college was established at Seward,

Nebr., in 1894. For many years high schools were operated in connection with the colleges. The student bodies were all male until the 1930s.

MISSION OUTREACH

As we learned in session 25, India was a primary target for Protestant mission efforts in the 1800s. The Missouri Synod also began work there in 1895, but it took nine years before Pastor Theodor Naether, one of the first Missouri Synod missionaries to India, baptized his first convert. By the mid-1900s the India Evangelical Lutheran Church had 50,000 members.

In Brazil growth was quicker. The Synod started a seminary at Porto Alegre in the early 1900s in response to the needs of the large number of German immigrants who had made their home in southern Brazil. The German language was used, of course (but, as in the United States, World War I led to the use of the prevailing language: Portuguese, in this case). The church has grown to almost 200,000 members in 400 congregations and stations.

OTHER LUTHERANS

Besides building a strong confessional Lutheran church body in America, Walther hoped to bring about a single united Lutheran church. To this end he sponsored free conferences with any and all who claimed to be Lutheran. Eventually (in 1872) a federation of synods called the Evangelical Lutheran Synodical Conference came into being, with Walther as its first president. It included the Ohio, Missouri, Norwegian, Wisconsin, and Slovak synods. Because of doctrinal disagreements, however, the Ohio and most of the Norwegian Synod soon withdrew.

Walther was unable to unite all Lutherans, leaving a lack of unity that prevails to this day. About half of the Lutherans in this country had belonged to the General Synod, which was started in 1820. Its leaders did not agree with some basic Lutheran teachings, such as those concerning Baptism and the Lord's Supper. They favored revivalism and tried to unite with certain existing sects that were anything but Lutheran.

In 1867 the Lutheran General Council, much more confessional than the General Synod, came into being. It did not, however, bring about a single Lutheran church body because of four areas of disagreement: exchanging pulpits with ministers of other denominations, communing non-Lutherans, allowing members to belong to secret societies, and holding to the doctrine of the millennium.

Dr. R. C. H. Lenski, a prominent theologian from another Lutheran group, gave his opinion of the Missouri Synod in the May 20, 1922, edition of the Ohio Synod publication, *Kirchenzeitung:*

If there ever was a strictly conservative Lutheran body, it surely is the Missouri Synod. Nevertheless, look at its growth! Here is a historical fact that refutes all talk trying to persuade us that we must be liberal, accommodate ourselves to the spirit of the time, etc., in order to win men and grow externally. The very opposite is seen in the Missouri Synod. Missouri has at all times been unyielding; it is so still. In this body the Scriptures and the Confessions have been, and still are, valued to their full import. There was no disposition to surrender any part of them. With this asset Missouri has been working in free America, which abounds in sects and religious confusion, and now exhibits its enormous achievements.

What so many regard as Missouri's weakness has in reality been its strength. This fact we might write down for our own remembrance. It is a mark of the pastors and leaders of the Missouri Synod that they never, aye never, tire of discussing doctrine on the basis of the Confessions and of Scriptures. That is one trait that may be called "The Spirit of Missouri."

FOR DISCUSSION

1. Compare the obstacles that might have prevented early growth in the Missouri Synod with obstacles that the church faces today.
2. Which factors contributed to the growth of the Synod?
3. Describe the early efforts to train pastors and teachers. Why was this training crucial to the development of the new synod?
4. Discuss the role of mission activities in the history of the Missouri Synod.
5. Why were the four issues confronting the General Council very important?
6. How, under God's blessings, can we overcome obstacles that seem likely to hinder growth?

A WORD FROM THE WORD

How can a young man keep his way pure? By living according to Your word. I seek You with all my heart; do not let me stray from Your commands. . . . I delight in Your decrees; I will not neglect Your Word.

Psalm 119:9–10, 16

SESSION 33

Kierkegaard, Barth, and Lewis

Be careful of your words.

Micah 7:5

In *Alice in Wonderland,* Humpty Dumpty tells Alice, "When *I* use a word, it means just what I choose it to mean— neither more or less."

"The question is," said Alice, "whether you *can* make words mean so many different things."

"The question is," said Humpty Dumpty, *"which is to be master*—that's all."

Words. In this session we will see how changing just a few words in familiar phrases produces skewed concepts of Christian doctrine.

SOREN KIERKEGAARD

He looked like a man on his way to the dentist. Parents would admonish stubborn boys by saying, "Don't be a Soren!" Soren Kierkegaard (1813–55) was born in Denmark. He was described as a tortured soul who regarded suffering as the basis of life. To him, God and humanity are on such different planes that the clash of time and eternity in time can only produce sufferings.

The institutional church was a constant target of Kierkegaard's verbal attacks. He advised a correspondent that if he failed to attend divine services, he would at least not sin in trying to fool God by identifying the kind of Christianity in his day with the true Christianity of the New Testament. Everything in Denmark, he said, could be called "Christian": Christian saloon-owners, Christian brothel-keepers. He denounced the established church as "an impudent indecency," with salaried ministers who were half worldly civil servants, proclaiming on Sundays the very opposite of what they did on Mondays.

We associate the term *existentialism* with Kierkegaard: one's existence is realized by inner decisions. Consciousness of sin must drive one to take "the leap of faith" from objective thinking to subjective belief. I must find a truth that is true *for myself* and for *my life,* rather than accept a system of outward faith.

Existentialists see human life as being basically a series of decisions that must be made, with no way of knowing conclusively what the correct choices are. The individual must continually decide what is true and what is false, what is right and what is wrong, which beliefs to accept and which to reject, what to do and what not to do. Yet, there are no objective standards or rules to which a person can turn for answers to problems of choice, for different standards supply conflicting advice. The individual must decide which standards to accept and which to reject.

Only after the general disillusionment that followed World War II did the writings of "the gloomy Dane" become known and accepted by many.

KARL BARTH

Karl Barth (1886–1968) was a Swiss-born theologian who was influenced by Kierkegaard. He came to the conclusion that the Word of God comes to us in three forms:

—Jesus Christ as the Word of God;
—the Word of God in preaching; and
—the Word of God in Scripture.

We certainly would agree that Jesus is the incarnate Word: **"In the beginning was the Word, and the Word was with God, and the Word was God. . . . The Word became flesh and made His dwelling among us"** (John 1:1, 14).

And Scripture is the Word of God. *But not without qualification,* says Barth. To him, Scripture is the witness to revelation, Jesus Christ, and a witness is not the same as that to which it witnesses. Fallible, erring people no different from us are witnesses, so what they have written cannot be identified with the Word of God.

This, of course, allows for mistakes—not just in historical and other secular matters, but even in religious or theological content. Revelation, Barth held, is dynamic, not static. The Bible is not the Word of God, but only *becomes* the Word of God where and when it functions as the word of a witness in an event. He proposed that the word *is* should be replaced with *was* or *will be* when we speak of the Bible as the Word of God.

In spite of this dangerous chipping away of the very norm and rule of Christian doctrines, Barth was opposed to liberalism. He taught that we and our works are under God's judgment, and our only hope is by

72

revelation through Jesus Christ and His cross and resurrection. We must set aside our pride and accept this revelation.

Because this sounded a bit like the orthodoxy of old, it was called "neoorthodoxy."

C. S. LEWIS

A recent popular defender of orthodox Christianity in the English-speaking world was a layman, Clive Staples Lewis (1898–1963), who was born in Belfast, Northern Ireland. Converted from unbelief to Christianity in 1929, he wrote in defense of Christian beliefs in a dignified but simple style and was called "the apostle to the skeptics." After reading his best-seller, *Mere Christianity,* Charles W. Colson, President Nixon's former lawyer, became a believer. Equally popular was his *Screwtape Letters.* Lewis could have become a very wealthy man, but instead he gave two-thirds of his income to charities.

Here is a sample of Lewis' forthright, logical argumentation:

I am trying here to prevent anyone saying the really foolish thing that people often say about Him: "I'm ready to accept Jesus as a great moral teacher, but I don't accept His claim to be God." That is the one thing we must not say. A man who is merely a man and said the sort of things Jesus said would not be a great moral teacher. He would either be a lunatic—on a level with the man who says he is a poached egg—or else He would be the Devil of Hell.

You must make your choice. Either this man was, and is, the Son of God: or else a madman or something worse. You can shut Him up for a fool, you can spit at Him and kill Him as a demon; or you can fall at His feet and call Him Lord and God. But let us not come with any patronizing nonsense about His being a great human teacher. He has not left that open to us. He did not intend to.

(From *Mere Christianity* [New York:MacMillan Publishing Co., 1943, 1945,1952].)

He tells of his own conversion:

You must picture me alone in that room in Magdalen, night after night, feeling, whenever my mind lifted even for a second from my work, the steady, unrelenting approach of Him whom I so earnestly desired not to meet. That which I greatly feared had at last come upon me. In the Trinity Term of 1929 I gave in, and admitted that God was God, and knelt and prayed: perhaps, that night, the most dejected and reluctant convert in all England. I did not then see what is now the most shining and obvious thing: the Divine humility which will accept a convert even on such terms. The Prodigal Son at least walked home on his own two feet. But who can duly adore that Love which will open the high gates to a prodigal who is brought in kicking, struggling, resentful, and darting his eyes in every direction for a chance to escape? The words, compelle intrare, *compel them to come in, have been so abused by wicked men that we shudder at them; but, properly understood, they plumb the depth of the Divine mercy. The hardness of God is kinder than the softness of men, and His compulsion is our liberation.*

(Excerpt from SURPRISED BY JOY, THE SHAPE OF MY EARLY LIFE by C. S. Lewis, copyright © 1956 by C. S. Lewis PTE Ltd. and renewed 1984 by Arthur Owen Barfield, reprinted by permission of Harcourt Brace & Company.)

FOR DISCUSSION

1. When only can truth be meaningful, according to Kierkegaard? How does existentialism run contrary to Scripture?
2. How does Barth's view of Scripture and the Word of God differ from that which confessional Lutherans hold?
3. In which way did Lewis destroy the notion that Jesus was a great moral teacher, but not God?
4. How was Lewis' conversion different from Luther's?
5. If you had a friend who was an unbeliever, would you use logical arguments in order to bring about his conversion? Why or why not?

A WORD FROM THE WORD

I do not hide Your righteousness in my heart; I speak of Your faithfulness and salvation. I do not conceal Your love and Your truth from the great assembly. Do not withhold Your mercy from me, O Lord; may Your love and Your truth always protect me.

Psalm 40:10–11

SESSION 34
Vatican II

I will surely gather all of you.

Micah 2:12

Vatican II (1962–65), a series of four sessions held in Rome, led to the publication of 16 documents that have become significant for the Roman Catholic Church: 2 dogmatic constitutions, 2 pastoral constitutions, 9 decrees, and 3 declarations.

John XXIII (pope 1958–63) called the meetings, and they were completed by Paul VI (pope 1963–78). Nearly 3,000 leaders of the Roman Catholic Church attended.

The 16 documents (about 100,000 words in all) dealt with many significant theological issues, but the people in the pew noticed one especially: For the first time in history, parts of the Mass were being said in English instead of Latin.

WORSHIP CHANGES

Previously people remained silent during the entire Mass. Now they were instructed to speak responses, sing congregational hymns, read appointed Scriptures out loud, and serve as "commentators." The priest no longer faced the altar with his back toward the people; he would face the people, standing behind a freestanding table placed before the ornate altar. Gradually the church offered both the bread and wine (body and blood) during Mass. (Previously people received only the bread [body].)

The Liturgy Constitution introduced a three-year lectionary, with selections the same as or similar to those now read in Lutheran churches; the sermon (homily) was given greater emphasis; and the Anointing of the Sick (formerly Extreme Unction) was to be given to those who are ill that the Lord "may lighten their suffering and save them." **James 5** was cited.

BIRTH CONTROL

Before Vatican II the Roman Catholic Church had taken the position that the Bible forbade birth control. They used the Sixth Commandment and the Onan account **(Genesis 38:8–10)** to support their position. They stated that the teaching was not directly based on Scripture, but that it was derived from natural law and by inference from early and medieval church writings.

Lay people showed an intense interest in this issue. Married couples did not always avoid pregnancies by using the rhythm method, the only birth-control method approved by the church.

On Oct. 4, 1965, Pope Paul addressed the United Nations' delegates. Millions watched and listened at their TV sets as he spoke about the sacred character of life. The pontiff admonished the representatives of the nations to find ways to furnish food for the growing population instead of encouraging the use of artificial means of birth control, which he called an irrational act (irrational for the nations; a sin for Catholics). In other words, Vatican II did not change the church's position on birth control: All types of contraceptives are forbidden, as are therapeutic abortions, even those done to save the life of a mother.

This action brought criticism, especially from outside the church and particularly since it came at a time when the Food and Agriculture organization stated that the world population was increasing 2 percent per year, while its food increased only 1 percent.

MARRIAGE

The council left unchanged the church's position on marriage. All valid marriages for Catholics had to be performed by priests in accordance with the rules of the church. Catholics could not marry non-Catholics unless by permission of a bishop, and the non-Catholic party would have to sign a pledge that the children would be raised Catholic. No marriages under Catholic auspices could be dissolved by divorce with the right of remarriage.

Some changes have occurred since Vatican II. On March 31, 1970, Pope Paul issued a statement, "Implementations of the Apostolic Letter on Mixed Marriages," which was approved by the National Council of Catholic Bishops later in the year. It reaffirms the position that the Catholic party must declare his (her) intention to do all in his (her) power to see to it that the children are raised Catholic. However, no declaration or promises are required of the non-Catholic party, though he (she) must be told of the promise made by the Catholic.

SOCIAL REFORM

Many people inside and outside the church praised the council's position on social reform. It focused attention on the dignity of the human being, the problems of atheism, and the role of the church in helping the needy. It called for the right of all people to have sufficient food, clothing, shelter, education, employment, a good reputation, respect of conscience, privacy, and freedom in religious matters.

The council condemned abortion, euthanasia, suicide, slavery, prostitution, unfair imprisonment, disgraceful working conditions, and the treatment of people as tools for profit.

The council's document also called for maintaining a distinction between error and persons in error, the equality of people, humane conditions for all, just wages, nondiscrimination of sexes in regard to employment, labor unions that would not work against the common good, the right to strike, benefits for the unemployed and disabled, and health care for all workers.

It also dealt with peace and war, renouncing violence and mass extermination. It upheld legitimate national defense and conscientious objectors. The council called the arms race an "utterly treacherous trap for humanity," and asked that efforts be made toward multilateral and controlled disarmament.

THE JEWS

Pope John had extended his arms to Jewish leaders who visited him in 1960, welcoming them with "I am Joseph, your brother."

The council's statements on Jews indicated that they were still "dear to God," even though their authorities had pressed for Christ's death. Jewish people today cannot be blamed for this. They should not be persecuted or discriminated against. The church looks forward to the day when "all peoples" will with a single voice address the Lord and serve Him.

OTHER CHRISTIANS

Many observers from other churches were under the impression that Vatican II had been called primarily to promote unity among all Christian churches. Pope Paul did say that whatever faults for the separation of Christendom were those of the Catholic Church, the latter asks for pardon for them both from God and from "our brothers." The council used language such as "remorse over our division," "divided Christians," and "our separated brethren."

Catholics have generally used "ecumenism" (from the Greek *oikoumene:* the whole inhabited world) to mean that all Christians are to submit to Rome. But the council did not go that far, although a part of the decree on ecumenism read:

Nevertheless, our separated brethren, whether considered as individuals or as Communities and Churches, are not blessed with that unity which Jesus Christ wished to bestow on all those whom He has regenerated and vivified into one body and newness of life—that unity which the holy Scriptures and the revered tradition of the Church proclaim. For it is through Christ's Catholic Church alone, which is the all-embracing means of salvation, that the fullness of the means of salvation can be obtained. It was to the apostolic college alone, of which Peter is the head, that we believe our Lord entrusted all the blessings of the New Covenant, in order to establish on earth the one Body of Christ into which all those should be fully incorporated, who already belong in any way to God's People (Decree on Ecumenism, no. 3).

FOR DISCUSSION

1. How did Vatican II improve the Mass?
2. Why do most Americans favor birth control? What position do you take? Why?
3. Suppose you fall in love with a Roman Catholic. How will you resolve the issues of marriage, birth control, and raising children?
4. React to the Social Reform document. Defend your position.
5. React to the position on ecumenism.
6. What evidence of God's grace do you find in your study of Vatican II? What evidence do you find of people resisting God's grace?

A WORD FROM THE WORD

Send forth Your light and Your truth, let them guide me; let them bring me to Your holy mountain, to the place where You dwell. Then will I go to the altar of God, to God, my joy and my delight.

Psalm 43:3–4

SESSION 35
Historical Criticism

Now is the time of their confusion.
Micah 7:4

Division among Christians at the time of the Reformation did not occur because of disagreement about the Bible. To Catholic, Lutheran, Reformed, and Anabaptist alike, Scripture was the Word of God. It was reliable and true. Denominations differed over how they interpreted that Word.

Some church leaders today, however, deny the truthfulness of what is written in the Bible.

BEGINNINGS

In session 27 we learned that a different approach to the Bible emerged when Friedrich Schleiermacher (1768–1834) fostered the notion that religion was based on "experience," which led to "dependence," but not on the written Scriptures. The Bible was regarded to be only a record of people "who had the Word of God." This subjective view led to the practice of researching Scripture like any other historical document. Theologians explained miracles in a way that would make them acceptable to human reason:

"Jesus didn't walk on the water, but on the shore."

"When Jesus shared a few loaves and fish, the 5,000 were so moved by His example that they also shared their lunches."

"Jesus 'swooned' on the cross, but He didn't actually die. The cool air in the tomb revived Him, and an earthquake moved the stone from the entrance."

One theologian, F. C. Baur (1792–1860), held that the early church was torn by a conflict between Peter and Paul and that those epistles that didn't reflect this conflict were not authentic. He held that only **Romans, Galatians,** and **1** and **2 Corinthians** were "genuine."

HISTORICAL CRITICISM

Webster's Third New International Dictionary defines higher criticism (another name for historical criticism) as the "literary-historical study of the Bible that seeks to determine such factors as authorship, date, place of origin, circumstances of composition, purpose of the author, and the historical credibility of each of the various biblical writings together with the meaning intended by their authors."

Most of these steps are not new; they constitute accepted procedures in studying the Scriptures. However, the act of determining the "historical credibility of each of the various biblical writings" places historical criticism at odds with the "Lutheran principle":

Holy Scripture remains the only judge, rule, and norm according to which as the holy touchstone all doctrines should and must be understood and judged as good or evil, right or wrong (Formula of Concord, Epitome, Rule and Norm, 7).

So far as "the meaning intended by their authors" is concerned, critics regard themselves to be in a better position to decide what the writer meant to say than the writer himself. What "meaning" can there be other than that which is expressed in the words of the writer? *The intent and purpose of historical criticism is to pass judgment on the accuracy and the completeness of the historical reports in the Bible.*

Edgar Krentz writes the following in *The Historical Critical Method* (Philadelphia: Fortress Press, 1975):

The biblical books became historical documents to be studied and questioned like any other ancient sources. The Bible was no longer the criterion for the writing of history; rather history had become the criterion for understanding the Bible. . . . The history it reported was no longer assumed to be everywhere correct. The Bible stood before criticism as defendant before judge (page 55).

(From *The Historical Critical Method* by Edgar Krentz, Fortress Press, © 1975. Used by permission of the publisher.)

TECHNIQUES

As just noted, not all of the elements employed in historical criticism are improper. First, we need to do *linguistic study.* The Bible contains documents written over a period of 1,600 years. While God inspired every word, each writer had his own vocabulary and used words in a unique way. One must take into account the historical situation, who the writer was, who the intended readers were, and the purpose of the writing.

Next we must carry out *textual criticism.* We do not

have the original manuscripts of the Biblical documents, so we must make a study of the available copies. "Variant readings" sometimes exist. Modern Bible translations usually list these at the bottom of pages or in the margin. In these instances textual criticism has been used to determine the most probable original text.

Form criticism assumes that the Biblical books came into existence as an amalgamation of old traditions and various smaller units (such as, in the case of the gospels, collections of miracle accounts, parables, and sayings of Jesus).

Out of this grew *redaction* (editing) *criticism.* If it's true, so goes the argument, that the text did not originate with what is now written in the Bible, but was pulled together from a number of sources, oral and written, the question must be asked, "Why did the editor choose to use this in his story and not something else?" What was his "theology"? What principles guided him?

Finally, *tradition criticism* results from "redaction criticism." Certain "traditions" appear more than once. Several writers spoke of the Exodus account. How did Moses use it in comparison with the way Joshua used it?

RESULTS

On the basis of available evidence, the critic decides what was actually said, what really happened, and what is true and not true about the text. "Available evidence" includes other ancient writings and the findings of archaeology.

For example, the account of Herod's slaughter of the innocents is recorded only once in the Bible **(Matthew 2)** and never referred to in other writings. Josephus, a Jewish historian who lived at the time of Christ, never mentions it. Nothing has ever been unearthed in Bethlehem to prove that it happened. Conclusion: It's a fabrication.

Similarly, Paul never mentions the virgin birth of Jesus in any of his epistles. Therefore, the critic could argue, it is suspect.

One of the most damaging results of historical criticism comes from the notion that later traditions were added to the gospels. The March 2, 1987, edition of *The Oregonian* carried the following story, under the headline, "Scholars Challenge 'Words' of Jesus":

SALEM—*A few days ago, in the week before Lent, a group of top-ranked biblical scholars meeting here determined that Jesus likely did not say the Seven Last Words attributed to him on the cross. . . . The seminar . . . was organized two years ago in an attempt to answer a basic question: which among all the sayings in the New Testament attributed to Jesus were most probably said by Jesus himself? . . .*

Scholars determined that it was unlikely that Jesus' conversations during the Last Supper were those recorded in the Bible or that he said the words attributed to him as prophecies of his death and resurrection. . . . Jesus' dying words, "My God, my God, why hast thou forsaken me," were considered inauthentic by a majority of the scholars, as was Jesus' plea, "Father, forgive them, for they know not what they do." The foretelling of Peter's betrayal, the prayers in the garden of Gethsemane against temptation, Jesus' promise to destroy the Jerusalem temple and his dialogue with the high priest after his arrest also are likely inauthentic and the addition of a later tradition. . . .

The Gospel accounts, while offering some clues to the historical Jesus, are imperfect historical documents, generally traced to the end of the first century, at least a generation after the death of Jesus in the year 30, according to biblical scholars.

(From *The Oregonian,* March 2, 1987. Used by permission.)

FOR DISCUSSION

1. What were some of the results of the subjective approach to Scripture taken around the time of Schleiermacher?
2. Why is the determination of the "historical credibility of each of the various biblical writings" in direct conflict with the confessional Lutheran view of Scripture?
3. What is the intent and purpose of historical criticism?
4. What legitimate study techniques are included in the historical-critical method?
5. What would you say to someone who does not believe in the resurrection of the body?

A WORD FROM THE WORD

You are my portion, O Lord; I have promised to obey Your words. I have sought Your face with all my heart; be gracious to me according to Your promise. I have considered my ways and have turned my steps to Your statutes.

Psalm 119:57–59

SESSION 36

Church Unions

I will surely gather all of you.

Micah 2:12

Look at the yellow pages of a telephone directory and you will find a bewildering choice of denominations. Is that good? Would it be better if we had only one church body? Would this create a more effective witness to non-Christians both in foreign countries and at home? What do you think?

COMING TOGETHER

Over the years Christian churches split into hundreds of denominations. We have looked at divisions created by theological differences. Others occurred because of political beliefs or national origins.

Many church leaders saw these divisions as an obstacle to missionary activities. In 1910 the World Missionary Conference was held at Edinburgh, Scotland. Eleven hundred delegates from every mission field in the world except South America met to consult about ways to cooperate and promote unity. John Mott was appointed to spearhead the operation. During the next few years he conducted 21 conferences in Asia alone.

Eventually, two kinds of cooperative efforts occurred among the Protestant churches: church federations and organic church unions. Because of doctrinal differences that prevented a united thrust on the mission fields, representatives from various denominations held meetings to discuss such matters and to seek agreement in enough beliefs so they could work together. These were called "Faith and Order" conferences.

WORLD COUNCIL OF CHURCHES

The first such conferences were held in Lausanne, Switzerland, and Edinburgh, Scotland, in 1927 and 1937, respectively. Invited were "all Christian communions throughout the world which confess our Lord Jesus Christ as God and Saviour."

The World Council of Churches was organized in 1948. It included Protestants and representatives of the Eastern Orthodox Church as a "fellowship of churches which accept our Lord Jesus Christ as God and Saviour." At a subsequent meeting in 1961, the statement was expanded: "The World Council of Churches is a fellowship of churches which confess the Lord Jesus Christ as God and Saviour according to the Scriptures and therefore seek to fulfill together their common calling to the glory of the one God, Father, Son, and Holy Spirit."

ORGANIC CHURCH UNIONS

Meanwhile some separate denominations began to merge. The United Church of Canada—including Methodists, Congregationalists, and some Presbyterians—came into being in 1925. In the United States, Methodists merged with other Methodist groups, Presbyterians with Presbyterians, Lutherans with Lutherans, and Baptists with Baptists. Abroad, Anglicans, Congregationalists, Methodists, Presbyterians, and Dutch Reformed became the Church of South India in 1947.

FAITH AND ORDER

Protestants, Catholics, and Orthodox met at Oberlin, Ohio, in 1957, where they adopted the following purpose: "To call the churches to the goal of visible unity in one faith and in one eucharistic fellowship expressed in worship and in common life in Christ and to advance toward that unity in order that the world may believe."

In July 1982 the representatives issued a document, *Baptism, Eucharist, and Ministry*. This was an attempt to reach agreement among the churches—to recognize each other's administration of Baptism, Communion, and the ordained ministry. They also addressed other goals: the affirmation of a common faith and the finding of ways to decide and act together.

LUTHERAN MERGER

Jan. 1, 1988, marked the merger of the 2.9 million-member Lutheran Church in America, the 2.3 million-member American Lutheran Church, and the 110,000-member Association of Evangelical Lutheran Churches into the Evangelical Lutheran Church of America (ELCA). It included almost 5.4 million of the 8.5 million Lutherans in the United States.

Many are asking, "Why didn't the Missouri Synod join in the merger?"

Despite years of doctrinal discussions with representatives of the church bodies that formed the ELCA, the Missouri Synod holds different views on the doctrine of Scripture, the meaning of subscription to the Confessions of the Lutheran church, and the measure of doctrinal agreement necessary for pulpit and altar fellowship with other denominations. These differences become especially visible in two practices: who should partake of the Lord's Supper and the ordination of women to the pastoral office.

Many professors in the seminaries of the merging Lutheran church bodies teach historical criticism, which we studied in our last session. They may say, for example, that the Bible is truthful and reliable *insofar as it reflects the religious experiences of the writers as they testified about Jesus.*

Regarding the Lutheran Confessions, the Missouri Synod accepts them *because* they rightly interpret and set forth the teachings of the Holy Scriptures. Some of those forming the new church speak of accepting them *insofar as* they rightly interpret Scripture. They hold that as long as we agree in the understanding of the Gospel as put in **John 3:16,** we can have diversity in other teachings.

These other teachings include a historical-critical view of **Genesis 1–3** and the acceptance of differing views of whether Christ's true body and blood are actually present with the consecrated bread and wine in the Lord's Supper. Recent efforts to commune and exchange pulpits with Episcopalians and Presbyterians (who officially deny the Real Presence) give evidences of doctrine and practice contrary to that maintained in the Lutheran Confessions.

This practice illustrates the "reconciled diversity" that exists among some Lutherans—a unity that transcends diversity, that agrees to live with doctrinal differences (illustrated also by the fact that at Minneapolis in February 1984 a statement of belief was almost changed from "Father, Son, and Holy Spirit" to "Creator, Redeemer, and Holy Spirit," because of the allegedly sexist language of "Father" and "Son"). The Missouri Synod believes that altar and pulpit fellowship should occur only when denominations agree on the authoritative teaching that actually goes on in the churches.

Is there nothing Lutherans can do together? We can continue to cooperate in external matters such as world relief and refugee settlement. We can also continue to discuss our differences.

As we do this, we have a wonderful opportunity to emphasize the primary business of the church—the Gospel of Jesus Christ.

Meanwhile, the Missouri Synod has held some discussions with the Wisconsin Evangelical Lutheran Synod (WELS). These denominations were in church fellowship from 1872 until 1961. Like Missouri, WELS accepts the Lutheran Confessions as right interpretations of Scripture.

WILL THERE EVER BE ONE "VISIBLE" CHURCH?

In the Nicene Creed we confess, "I believe in one holy Christian and apostolic church" (which is the total number of those who believe in Christ.)

In **Romans 12:5** Paul writes, **"In Christ we who are many form one body."**

In **Ephesians 4:4–5** he writes, **"There is one body and one Spirit . . . one Lord, one faith, one baptism."**

God certainly desires unity. But so long as the devil, our sinful flesh, and the sinful world remain, we can expect divisions in Christendom, in society, and in families. Even so, God desires that we pray and work for unity: **"I appeal to you, brothers, in the name of our Lord Jesus Christ, that all of you agree with one another so that there may be no divisions among you and that you may be perfectly united in mind and thought"** (1 Corinthians 1:10).

FOR DISCUSSION

1. Tell how divisions among Christians hamper mission work.
2. How does the *Baptism, Eucharist, and Ministry* document propose a solution to the denominational problem?
3. Why did the Missouri Synod not become involved in the Lutheran merger?
4. How can divided Christians carry out Christ's command to **"Go and make disciples of all nations" (Matthew 28:19)?**
5. What are some of the major challenges the Missouri Synod faces today?

A WORD FROM THE WORD

Your statutes are wonderful; therefore I obey them. The unfolding of Your words gives light; it gives understanding to the simple. . . . Direct my footsteps according to Your Word.

Psalm 119:129–30, 133a

SESSION 37

The Charismatic Movement

I am filled with power, with the Spirit of the Lord.
Micah 3:8

Mrs. Miller never misses church. She is active in the same denomination in which her parents and their parents held membership. But one evening every week she meets with a local group of women from Catholic, Lutheran, and Episcopal churches for prayer, speaking in tongues, and healing.

Millions of 20th-century Christians claim loyalty to their own church, but also attend charismatic meetings and services with people of other denominations. This practice is typical of those who have come to be known as "the charismatics."

RETURN OF THE SPIRIT?

According to John Wesley, a "still higher salvation," a "second blessing" of the Holy Spirit, was attainable after a person was "born again." This would be a sudden transformation, the soul would be renewed, and perfect love would replace sin. While Wesley himself never claimed he had the "second blessing," his followers pursued the idea after his death. Phoebe Palmer, for example, in *Guide to Christian Perfection,* held that entire holiness was a result of claiming God's promise: the baptism of the Holy Spirit.

By the late 1800s formality had become a problem for some in the Methodist Church, and it no longer stressed the doctrine of total sanctification. Revivalists Charles Finney and Dwight Moody preached it, but the masses never really accepted it.

Those who did teach this doctrine held that three steps had to be taken in order to reach the level of holiness: justification, cleansing, and the "second blessing"—the baptism of the Holy Spirit. Practices of healing and speaking in tongues finally brought about a rift among Methodists as the Holiness groups resisted church authority.

Many Catholics have joined the movement, but they did not separate themselves from the institutional church. Pope Paul VI gave them his unofficial blessing, as did John Paul II in 1981.

Today's charismatic movement differs from Pentecostalism. The latter, numbering some 20 groups, came into being at the beginning of the 20th century. Prominent were the Nazarenes, Assemblies of God, Church of God, Church of God in Christ, Foursquare Gospel Church, United Pentecostal Church, and the Pentecostal Holiness Church. While each held unique beliefs, all emphasized "speaking in tongues" as evidence of "the baptism of the Holy Spirit."

CHARISMATIC BELIEFS

Charismatics believe that the Holy Spirit has given them direct revelations—as they claim first-century Christians possessed, such as speaking in tongues, gifts of healing and prophecy, and even raising the dead. For them the experience of the "second baptism" with the Spirit takes precedence over the authority of Scripture. Many hold that the Gospel is incomplete without the assurance given in the "second baptism."

Many charismatics give special attention to speaking in tongues, often in a language that needs interpretation. When we read **1 Corinthians 14,** however, it becomes evident that Paul does not rank the gift of tongues all that highly and that it caused problems in the congregation. It should also be kept in mind that the disciples on Pentecost spoke in languages already in existence: **"All of them were filled with the Holy Spirit and began to speak in other tongues as the Spirit enabled them.... When they heard this sound, a crowd came together in bewilderment, because each one heard them speaking in his own language" (Acts 2:4, 6).**

Charismatic leaders like Demos Shakarian (founder of the Full Gospel Businessmen's Fellowship International) believe that the Spirit must be received "above all gifts."

This is dangerous. If I am troubled over my sins, I am directed to my own inner spiritual estate and not to Christ. This will lead either to pride or despair.

Charismatic claims about blessings received in the (second) baptism of the Spirit imply that we cannot receive certain powers and blessings through the Word and sacraments. But Luther, in the Large Catechism, writes:

In Baptism we are given the grace, Spirit, and power to suppress the old man so that the new may come forth and grow strong.

Therefore Baptism remains forever. Even though we fall from it and sin, nevertheless we always have access to it so that we may again subdue the old man. But we need not again have the water poured over us. Even if we were immersed in water a hundred times, it would nevertheless be only one baptism, and the effect and signification of Baptism would continue and remain. Repentance, therefore, is nothing else than a return and approach to Baptism, to resume and practice what had earlier been begun but abandoned.

I say this to correct the opinion, which has long prevailed among us, that our Baptism is something past which we can no longer use after falling again into sin. We have such a notion because we regard Baptism only in the light of a work performed once for all. . . .

Thus we see what a great and excellent thing Baptism is, which snatches us from the jaws of the devil and makes God our own, overcomes and takes away sin and daily strengthens the new man, always remains until we pass from this present misery to eternal glory.

Therefore let everybody regard his Baptism as the daily garment which he is to wear all the time. Every day he should be found in faith and amid its fruits, every day he should be suppressing the old man and growing up in the new. If we wish to be Christians, we must practice the work that makes us Christians. But if anybody falls away from his Baptism let him return to it. As Christ, the mercy-seat, does not recede from us or forbid us to return to him even though we sin, so all his treasures and gifts remain. As we have once obtained forgiveness of sins in Baptism, so forgiveness remains day by day as long as we live, that is, as long as we carry the old Adam about our necks (Baptism, 76–80, 83–86).

WORDS OF CAUTION

Already at the time of the Reformation, Lutherans were warned about the notion of "direct revelation":

In short, enthusiasm clings to Adam and his descendants from the beginning to the end of the world. It is a poison implanted and inoculated in man by the old dragon, and it is the source, strength, and power of all heresy, including that of the papacy and Mohammedanism. Accordingly, we should and must constantly maintain that God will not deal with us except through the external Word and sacrament. Whatever is attributed to the Spirit apart from such Word and sacrament is of the devil. (Smalcald Articles, III, viii, 9-10.)

A 1977 document from the Commission on Theology and Church Relations of The Lutheran Church—Missouri Synod (*The Lutheran Church and the Charismatic Movement, Guidelines for Pastors and Congregations*) gives seven topics with a theological basis for their evaluation:

1. Spiritual gifts are not to be considered means of grace.
2. God has not promised to reveal His will to us directly and immediately (without means), as for example through visions and dreams.
3. Special signs and wonders are not indispensable guarantees that the Spirit of God dwells within an individual.
4. Faith in Christ does not necessarily eliminate illness and affliction from the life of a Christian.
5. Christian certainty is not based on "feeling" but on the objective promises of the Gospel.
6. "Baptism with the Spirit" is not a basis for church fellowship.
7. The gift of the Holy Spirit does not necessarily include extraordinary spiritual gifts.

FOR DISCUSSION

1. What are key beliefs of the charismatics?
2. Why do you think so many people have become involved in the charismatic movement?
3. Discuss the relationship between baptism by water and baptism of the Spirit.
4. Why are the charismatic doctrines dangerous to our salvation?
5. How would you witness to someone who claims to be a charismatic?
6. According to **1 Corinthians 12:7** and **14:5,** why does God give spiritual gifts to His people? What problem with the gift of speaking in tongues existed in the Corinthian congregation according to **chapter 14?**

A WORD FROM THE WORD

Search me, O God, and know my heart; test me and know my anxious thoughts. See if there is any offensive way in me, and lead me in the way everlasting.

Psalm 139:23–24

SESSION 38

The Television Evangelists

As for the prophets who lead My people astray, if one feeds them, they proclaim "peace"; if he does not, they prepare to wage war against him.
Micah 3:5

Mrs. Johnson never misses church. Like Mrs. Miller, she is active in the same denomination in which her parents and their parents held membership. But before she attends the late Sunday morning service, she tunes in her favorite TV evangelist. Then, when she sits down to write a check to be placed in her offering envelope, she also writes one for the work of the "electronic church" and drops it off in the mailbox on her way to church.

Years ago some people predicted that in the latter part of the 20th century it would be a common practice for Americans to hold membership in two separate denominations. As noted in the last section, it has come to pass, in a sense.

ORAL ROBERTS

Oral Roberts began a television ministry during the early 1950s. He has appealed especially to individuals who desire healing from some physical ailment. Gifts he has received from that ministry have enabled him to found Oral Roberts University and a $15 million church (Church on the Rock) that seats over 5,000 people. Roberts has also gained personal economic prosperity through his TV ministry.

BILLY GRAHAM

Though he does not have a regular TV ministry like Oral Roberts or Robert Schuler, the televised portions of his crusades qualify Billy Graham as a TV evangelist. Many consider Graham to be the most successful evangelist in history.

The Billy Graham Evangelistic Association, organized in 1950, began "The Hour of Decision" radio program, featuring him as main speaker. During succeeding years Graham traveled throughout the world, holding mass rallies, or "crusades," calling for individual "decisions for Christ." Those who came forward were assigned to local churches for a follow-up ministry.

At the 1957 New York crusade close to 57,000 persons "decided" for Christ after a two-year preparatory program costing $2½ million. The money was spent on 650 billboards, 40,000 phone-dial cards with the words "Pray for Billy Graham," and twice-daily TV appearances by his manager.

Graham became a frequent guest at the White House, becoming close to presidents Johnson and Nixon. His sermons and writings were simple and direct:

The question that comes to many minds is this: Just what must I do actually to receive Christ?...

First, you must recognize that God loved you so much that He gave His Son to die on the cross. "For God so loved the world, that He gave His only begotten Son, that whosoever believeth in Him should not perish, but have everlasting life" (John 3:16). "The Son of God . . . loved me, and gave Himself for me" (Galatians 2:20).

Second, you must repent of your sins. Jesus said: "Except ye repent, ye shall . . . perish" (Luke 13:3). He said: "Repent . . . and believe" (Mark 1:15). As John Stott, pastor of All Souls Church in London, wrote: "The faith which receives Christ must be accompanied by the repentance which rejects sin." Repentance does not mean simply that you are to be sorry for the past. To be sorry is not enough; you must repent. This means that you must turn your back on sins.

Third, you must receive Jesus Christ as Savior and Lord. "But as many as received Him, to them He gave power to become the sons of God, even to them that believe on His name" (John 1:12). This means that you accept God's offer of love, mercy, and forgiveness. This means that you accept Jesus Christ as your only Lord and your only Savior. This means that you cease struggling and trying to save yourself. You trust Him completely, without reservation, as your Lord and Saviour.

Fourth, you must confess Christ publicly. Jesus said: "Whosoever therefore shall confess me before men, him will I confess also before My Father which is in heaven" (Matthew 10:32). This confession carries with it the idea of a life so lived in front of your fellowmen that they will see a difference. It also means that you acknowledge with your mouth the Lord Jesus: "If thou shalt confess with thy mouth the Lord Jesus, and shalt believe in thine heart that God hath raised him from the dead, thou shalt be saved" (Romans 10:9). It is extremely important that when you receive Christ you tell someone else about it just as soon as possible. This gives you strength and courage to witness.

It is important that you make your decision and your commitment to Christ now. "Now is the accepted time . . . now is the day of salvation" (2 Corinthians 6:2). If you are willing to repent of your sins and to receive Jesus Christ as your Savior, you can do it now.

(From *World Aflame* by Billy Graham, copyright © 1965, Word, Inc., Dallas, Texas. All rights reserved.)

Graham's message of sin and grace has reached millions. Christians of other denominations rejoice because he refers those who answer "the altar call" to local churches. Graham also regards the Bible as God's Word; Jesus Christ as the true God-Man who died, rose, and will return; and heaven, hell, angels, and the devil as really existing.

But orthodox Christians cannot agree with Graham's doctrine of the free will. He gives an example of his teaching (that we are capable of believing by our own power) on page 154 of *World Aflame,* where he refers to Lydia's conversion: "She opened her heart, believed, and was converted without struggle or conflict." But the text reads, **"The Lord opened her heart to respond to Paul's message" (Acts 16:14).**

Secondly, Graham demands "*you* must recognize," "*you* must repent," "*you* must receive," "*you* must confess." However, his Scripture quotations are the vehicles through which *the Spirit* works.

Thirdly, Graham avoids mentioning Baptism and the Lord's Supper.

Finally, Graham espouses premillennialism: "Some of the ultimate results of the coming of Christ are clearly outlined in the Bible. . . . First, peace will be established on the earth. . . . Second, our social institutions will be reconstructed. . . . Third, Christ will restore nature to its original state. . . . Fourth, Christ will make righteousness international. . . . Fifth, Christ will reproduce the will of God on earth" (*World Aflame,* pp. 202–13). He rejects the traditional teaching of the Last Judgment: "The Bible knows nothing of a general judgment in which all men appear before God at the same time." He calls **Matt. 25:31–46** a "judgment of the nations" (*ibid.,* pp. 137–38).

ROBERT SCHULER

Some TV evangelists follow the philosophy of Norman Vincent Peale, who advocated universalism and the cult of "positive thinking." Self-confidence and the "Emerson motto" ("They conquer who believe they can") formed the basis of his teaching. He used Bible verses for "thought conditioners," and saw Jesus Christ as an "unseen partner" and an "advisor." The word *sin* never appears in his book, *The Power of Positive Thinking for Young People* (Englewood Cliffs, NJ: Prentice-Hall, 1952), nor does he make any reference to Christ as Savior from sin, despite the many moral problems with which he deals.

The message of Robert Schuler is much the same ("Tough times never last, but tough people do"). He promotes what he calls "possibility thinking."

Advertising on Schuler's book, *Tough Times Never Last, But Tough People Do* (Nashville: Thomas Nelson Publishers, 1983), sums up his emphasis on self:

"No matter what your problem—whether it's unemployment, poor health, destructive habits, loneliness, fear, or anything else that blocks your success—you can turn your negative into a positive. Name your problem, and you name your possibility." As in books by Peale, this volume is filled with examples of persons who, by following certain principles of optimism, achieved what at first were unreachable goals.

Schuler advises his audience to be positive, assured that they are able to solve their problems. He does not ever mention the elements that are part and parcel of failures: sin, Satan, our flesh. Nor does he identify Christ as the remedy. He calls prayer the "power that pulls everything together successfully" (with no reference to praying in Christ's name).

FOR DISCUSSION

1. What do you like about Billy Graham's preaching?
2. In what areas does Graham's theology disagree with Scripture?
3. Of the three evangelists, who in your opinion is closest to Scripture? What criteria did you use to arrive at that opinion?
4. In what ways are TV religious programs a blessing for homebound persons? What problems can arise for these people, however?
5. Evaluate the role of TV evangelists in your world.

A WORD FROM THE WORD

I proclaim righteousness in the great assembly; I do not seal my lips, as You know, O Lord. I do not hide Your righteousness in my heart; I speak of Your faithfulness and salvation. I do not conceal Your love and Your truth from the great assembly.
Psalm 40:9–10

SESSION 39
The New Evangelicals

We will walk in the name of the Lord.
Micah 4:5

When Terry Bradshaw arrived in Pittsburgh to lead the Steelers to several successful seasons of pro football, he hosted a breakfast for the local clergy. "I am a Christian who happens to be a quarterback," he told them.

This expression, which places the emphasis on belief rather than professional skills, is still a hallmark of "born again" persons in tightly knit circles who have become known as the New Evangelicals.

A "CHRISTIAN LIFE-STYLE"

The New Evangelicals allow for diversity in doctrinal emphases, so it's difficult to construct a systematic theology that embraces the total spectrum. When we look for a common element in the "old-fashioned religion" of Jerry Falwell and the "possibility thinking" of Robert Schuler, we find two things, at least: a lifestyle of piety and certain catchphrases gleaned from the literature of the movement's leaders.

The New Evangelical movement seems to suggest that we accomplish a "Christian" life-style by
—immersing ourselves in Christian bookstore products, and
—using "Christian" phone directories, car dealers, contractors, etc.

LONELY AND AIMLESS

The mood of the "lonely and aimless '80s" resulted from many varied and complex forces. Technological developments such as cable TV, VCRs, and personal computers, while promising a better quality of life, have also added to the isolation in which Americans live their lives. Perhaps you have seen joggers and others wearing a portable radio or tape player as they circulate, unaware of the passing scene and the people in it.

As never before, many and strong forces contribute to loneliness. The average American moves 14 times in a lifetime. Family members who were once on hand to offer personal support in critical times are miles away. Also, more and more single parents must somehow hold down a job and raise a child or two, who come home to an empty house. The advertising of telephone companies focuses on this very thing: dial Grandma and it's like she's in the next room.

The New Evangelicals emphasize the "friendliness factor" in their public worship experiences. Standard procedures include greeters at the door, get-acquainted rituals with your neighbor in the next pew before the service starts, name cards on the lapel, a cheery phone call, and a letter of welcome as followups. Unlike celebrations among confessional Lutherans, all are welcome to join in the bread-and-wine fellowship meal which the ushers distribute to members and guests alike.

While basically Fundamentalist in doctrine, the New Evangelicals strive to develop the Christian message into modern thought forms, while still battling the evils of the present world. They work to make their brand of belief and life-style "respectable."

MEDIA AND LIFE-STYLE

Many New Evangelicals concentrate on the use of the media, especially in the area of "Christian music."

Almost every community in the country has a local "Christian" radio station. As early as 1979 one of every seven TV stations in the country was "Christian" owned. New "Christian" stations come into existence at the rate of one a month. Some question their use of the techniques of secular advertising:

The point is to make the picture so appealing that the customer wants to see himself within the frame. Health, wealth, youth (or at least youthful age), sharp clothes, exuberant optimism. Is the product Coca-Cola or Christ? It's hard to tell. (From Virginia S. Owens, *The Total Image: Selling Jesus in the Modern Age* [Grand Rapids: Eerdmans, 1980], p. 105. Used by permission.)

Their literature and tapes touch virtually every subject:

The proliferation of religious books, however, has come about not because more and better books are being written but because there is a statistically predictable market for them. Cookbooks, diet books, exercise books, sex books, money books, sports books, psychology books. Every element that can be abstracted from secular culture to bolster the Christian culture. We are awash in a sea of supposedly Christian information. Thus have we succeeded in trivializing the infinite. (Owens, p. 76. Used by permission.)

Thus, the New Evangelicals emphasize life-style. While they carry, read, and quote the Bible, they do it with a smile and a hug. Seminars, conferences, and workshops replace catechisms as the primary method of teaching Christianity.

Among some people the "Christian life-style" dominates the entire day.

Christians can now spend an entire day within an evangelical context, even as they continue to function in the broader secular culture. In the morning, husband and wife wake up to an evangelical service on their local Christian owned and operated radio station. The husband leaves for work where he will start off his day at a businessman's prayer breakfast. The evangelical wife bustles the children off to their Christian Day School. At midmorning she relaxes in front of the TV set and turns on her favorite Christian soap opera. Later in the afternoon, while the Christian husband is attending a Christian business seminar, and the children are engaged in an after-school Christian sports program, the Christian wife is doing her daily shopping at a Christian store, recommended in her Christian Business Directory. In the evening the Christian family watches the Christian World News on TV and then settles down for dinner. After dinner, the baby-sitter arrives—she is part of a baby-sitter pool from the local church. After changing into their evening clothes, the Christian wife applies a touch of Christian makeup, and then they're off to a Christian nightclub for some socializing with Christian friends from the local church. They return home later in the evening and catch the last half hour of the "700 Club," the evangelical Johnny Carson Show. The Christian wife ends her day reading a chapter or two from Marabel Morgan's best-selling Christian book, The Total Woman. *Meanwhile her husband leafs through a copy of* Inspiration *magazine, the evangelical* Newsweek, *before they both retire for the evening.*

(From *The Emerging Order, God in the Age of Scarcity,* by Jeremy Rifkin, with Ted Howard. New York: G. Putnam's Sons, © 1979, p. 125.)

"HOW TO" THEOLOGY

The literature of the movement is saturated with suggestions for the Christian life, usually with one or more Scripture passages as touchstones: "How to . . . give, forgive, be a peacemaker, be obedient, cope with suffering, control the body, handle money, get closer to others, etc." When the Gospel appears, it fails to show God rescuing us from death and reconciling us to Himself. Instead we see Christ freeing us to reach our full potential. Thus, even the Gospel becomes another "how to," and not the motivating source of Christian living.

It's too early to tell how the movement will affect mainline churches, or what shape it will yet take as it matures. The use of the Bible primarily as a reference book with brief answers to all of life's complexities may not last long.

FOR DISCUSSION

1. Why does New Evangelicalism appeal to people in our time?
2. Do people appear friendly and loving at the church you attend? Do you think this is important? Why or why not?
3. How do the New Evangelicals teach Christianity?
4. How does the life-style of the New Evangelicals affect the average day of a devoted follower?
5. In what way is the true Gospel lost in much of New Evangelicalism literature?
6. What parts of the New Evangelicals' message do you think are most needed in your congregation? How is this message related to the Gospel of Christ? What can we learn from that message—how can we proclaim the Gospel more effectively?

A WORD FROM THE WORD

When we were overwhelmed by sins, You forgave our transgressions. . . . You answer us with awesome deeds of righteousness . . . . Where morning dawns and evening fades You call forth songs of joy.

Psalm 65:3, 5, 8

SESSION 40

Concluding Activities for Unit 4

TERMS

Write brief descriptions of the terms that follow:
1. Prussian Union
2. Synodical Conference
3. Existentialism
4. Vatican II
5. Ecumenism
6. Historical Criticism
7. Organic Church Union
8. World Council of Churches
9. Charismatics
10. Electronic Church
11. New Evangelicalism
12. "How to" Theology

SHORT ANSWERS

Write a short answer to each of the following questions:
1. Why did the Saxons leave Germany?
2. What problems could have prevented the early growth of the Missouri Synod?
3. How did C. S. Lewis destroy the notion that Jesus was a great moral teacher, but not God?
4. Which changes in the Mass caught the attention of American Catholics after Vatican II?
5. What is the intent and purpose of historical criticism?
6. Why didn't the Missouri Synod join other Lutheran church bodies in the 1988 merger?
7. Which supernatural gifts do charismatics claim to have?
8. How do charismatic teachings endanger one's salvation?
9. Which Biblical doctrine does Billy Graham sacrifice in his insistence on "decisions for Christ"?
10. Why does New Evangelicalism appeal to people today?
11. How does the life-style of the New Evangelicals affect the average devoted follower's day?

UNIT 5
The Lutheran Church— Missouri Synod Today

An article in the December 1982 issue of the *Saturday Evening Post* told about The Lutheran Church—Missouri Synod (LCMS):

For "people who never got out of the Bible," the Missouri Synod Lutherans are employing surprisingly progressive methods to further their traditional ways.... None of these members would deny that their church has a great respect for its roots, its confessional heritage, its tradition. But its unique character can be seen in the way in which it is both innovative and traditionalist—a seeming contradiction, but for the Missouri Synod a way of life that can be documented throughout its 135-year history....

Unobtrusively, these quiet Lutherans continue, largely off the beaten path, a remarkable entity. The grace of God, the blending of cultures and the commitment to worldwide outreach, democracy and the blessings of benign technology have enabled them to carry on an extensive and highly effective ministry.

(Reprinted with permission of the Saturday Evening Post Society, a division of BFL & MS, Inc., © 1987).

While we have already touched on the Missouri Synod in former sessions, these final four will concentrate on the Synod's titanic doctrinal struggle, mission outreach, educational institutions, and social ministry.

SESSION 41

Doctrinal Controversy in The Lutheran Church—Missouri Synod

When the foundations are being destroyed, what can the righteous do?

Psalm 11:3

"About the Virgin Birth of our Lord: I would go into one class and hear that this was a biological fact and that by no means could we entertain anything other than a literal view of what Matthew and Luke report. I went into another class and I heard that the New Testament really presents different positions on the Virgin Birth. Mark or Paul did not mention it; so, in fact, although one can choose to believe in the Virgin Birth, he can also choose not to believe, in the sense that he takes it as a theological embellishment by the early church by an early redactor [editor]. . . .

"The same was said about the existence of angels."

So stated a former student of Concordia Seminary, St. Louis, during a special hearing in 1973.

COMMITTEE 3

The president of The Lutheran Church—Missouri Synod appointed a special committee (Committee 3) to gather information and make recommendations in connection with accusations that had been made against certain professors at Concordia Seminary, St. Louis. The committee spent over 100 hours reviewing faculty documents and interviewing students, graduates, faculty members, and others from the seminary. The hearings led to the presentation of a long resolution to the Synod at its July 1973 convention in New Orleans. The resolution read, in part:

Resolved, that the Synod repudiate that attitude toward Holy Scripture, particularly as regards its authority and clarity, which reduces to theological opinion or exegetical questions matters which are in fact clearly taught in Scripture (e.g., facticity of miracle accounts and their details; historicity of Adam and Eve as real persons; the fall of Adam and Eve into sin as a real event, to which original sin and its imputation upon all succeeding generations of mankind must be traced; the historicity of every detail in the life of Jesus as recorded by the evangelists; predictive prophecies in the Old Testament which are in fact Messianic; the doctrine of angels; the Jonah account, etc.).

NEW ORLEANS CONVENTION

The New Orleans convention may have been the most crucial of all the 50 regular conventions of the Missouri Synod that were held in its 136-year history. Would the three-million-member church body follow other major denominations in changing its view of the Bible? While a significant number of the approximately 1,100 delegates did not favor the resolution, the majority prevailed.

The convention was disrupted at one point when several hundred delegates marched to the podium, bringing along slips of paper with their names written on them and singing the first stanza of "The Church's One Foundation" over and over.

Members of the faculty were given the opportunity to speak. The seminary president stated that he forgave the delegates. A resolution to remove him from office was withdrawn. The Missouri Synod made headlines and front page news as never before.

WHAT LED UP TO IT

Evidence shows that historical criticism had found a place in some of the Synod's educational institutions years earlier. A basic religion textbook used at one of the teachers colleges branded the birth stories of Jesus as not being compatible and set forth the notion that Matthew had developed his own elaborate account of the Resurrection. **Matthew 18:18,** it claimed, was never spoken by Jesus, but was added by the early church in order to justify the church's authority.

Some date the doctrinal problems as far back as the 1930s. By the 1960s the major issue had to do with the nature of the authority of Scripture: in which way was it God's Word, and how should it be interpreted?

Because the president of the Synod "has the supervision regarding the doctrine and the administration of . . . all such as are employed by the Synod" (LCMS Constitution, Art. XI, B, 1, b), those who held the office made efforts to resolve the problems, mostly by holding meetings of various professors and officials. However, not until April 20, 1970, did the president, who had been elected in 1969, take steps to initiate an official investigation. In a letter to the St. Louis seminary Board of Control he announced that he had decided to appoint a "factfinding" committee:

For several years, many in our fellowship have been disturbed by departures from our Synod's doctrinal position on the part of individuals serving in various capacities within our church. Individuals and Boards continue to receive requests from individuals, congregations, conferences, and even entire Districts, to deal constructively with the situation. Although officials and boards have no doubt made sincere efforts through the years to remedy the situation, the problem seems to be increasing instead of decreasing.

Events in recent months have convinced me that my constitutional responsibility as President requires that I take decisive action on this matter. I consider such action necessary to help the members and institutions in Synod remain faithful to the Word of God and the Lutheran Confessions, to assist the Synod in the achievement of the purpose for which it was organized, and to protect the workers in institutions of the Synod from unfounded or unjust allegations.

In view of the responsibilities placed upon me . . . I am appointing a Fact Finding Committee. This Committee is directly responsible to the President of the Synod.

On Sept. 1, 1972, the extensive findings of the committee were sent throughout the Synod. The summary reads, in part, that there is evidence of "a false doctrine of the nature of the Holy Scriptures coupled with methods of interpretation which effectively erode the authority of the Scriptures" (*Report of the Synodical President,* p. 25).

SEMINEX

After the New Orleans convention, the seminary president was charged with allowing and fostering false doctrine, and was eventually removed from the Synod's ministerium. Early in 1974 most of the faculty joined him in a "walk-out." They were accompanied by several hundred students, leaving behind 80 young men and 5 professors. Those who left formed a new seminary ("Seminary-in-Exile," better known as "Seminex") and tried, with the help of several District presidents, to place their graduates in the Synod's congregations.

Subsequently, four District presidents were removed from office by the president of the Synod for violating the Constitution. This led 182 congregations to break ties with the Synod and to form a new church body, the Association of Evangelical Lutheran Churches, numbering about 110,000 members.

By 1979 the St. Louis seminary enrollment had once again grown to 560. Seminex disbanded in the early 1980s.

While the Synod regained its historic doctrinal base, the controversy divided families—a situation that continued to persist. Many young men "caught in the middle" ended their careers before they began.

FOR DISCUSSION

1. What attitude toward Scripture did Committee 3 ask the 1973 convention of the Missouri Synod to condemn?
2. Discuss the significance of the 1973 convention of the Missouri Synod. How have you been affected by actions that occurred there?
3. What factors led to the formation of Seminex?
4. Discuss the relationship between the group that left the Missouri Synod (Association of Evangelical Lutheran Churches) and the Lutheran union described in session 36.
5. Compare the doctrinal position of the Missouri Synod today with that of the same body just before its 1973 convention.
6. Students tend to be loyal to their teachers. What would you do if a teacher you like were accused of teaching false doctrine?
7. What evidence of God's grace do you find in the events of this session?

A WORD FROM THE WORD

I have chosen the way of truth; I have set my heart on Your laws. I hold fast to Your statutes, O Lord; do not let me be put to shame. I run in the path of Your commands, for You have set my heart free.
Psalm 119:30–32

SESSION 42

Mission Activities of The Lutheran Church—Missouri Synod

Sing praises to the Lord; . . . proclaim among the nations what He has done.

Psalm 9:11

In July 1980, 32 families gathered for a closing service of worship at the Link Care Center in Fresno, CA, where they had just completed training as overseas missionaries for the LCMS. At the service, centered on **Isaiah 66:19 ("they will proclaim My glory among the nations"),** a large wooden cross was brought to the altar from the rear of the chapel by handing it overhead, every person touching it and singing, "Lift High the Cross."

"With God's help and His blessing we are determined to plant the cross of Jesus Christ in every country and nation to which the Lord is sending us," they pledged in unison, as each missionary placed on the altar a map of the country he would be entering.

INTO ALL THE WORLD

Since that time, mission work has been started by the LCMS in 25 "nations" (groups of people within "countries") and in 3 countries where less than 10 percent of the population is Christian.

Never before has the church faced so great a mission challenge. With a rapidly growing population and with opportunities to communicate through mass media, Christians are using many ways to respond to the Savior's Great Commission. The world today contains 5 billion people living in 223 countries made up of about 22,000 people groups. By the year 2020 the population is expected to reach the 8.5 billion mark.

We live in a world where 5,445 languages are spoken, but only 1,811 have an alphabet and can be written. Only one out of every four persons is a Christian. Mobility of the people complicates mission work. During the past 20 years a vast number of people from Asia, Africa, and the Caribbean have made their home in North America. Many came from 37 countries not open to Christian missionaries.

HERE AT HOME

When we speak of "missions" today, we cannot restrict the term to mean work overseas, important as that is. North America is now a mission field with 500 ethnic groups, an equal number of American Indian tribes, 23 million Hispanics, and 26 million blacks. Florida alone is the home of half a million Cubans.

The *American Indian* is not just a vanishing figure in history; his descendants are very much alive and in need of the saving Gospel. The Northern Cheyenne in Montana speak of the prophecy concerning the buffalo. Long ago Sweet Medicine, an old tribal "prophet," predicted that someday the buffalo would become extinct. This would bring about great suffering for the dwindling tribe. But he also said that the buffalo would return and the Cheyenne would again see good days. It happened as he predicted. Recently an LCMS layman from Seward, Nebr., gave the Montana tribe a herd of buffalo. According to Sweet Medicine, a new way of life would come from the white man when the buffalo return. This "new way," many Cheyenne have come to believe, may be the Gospel of Jesus Christ.

Hispanics will soon be the largest minority group in the United States. Some estimate that by 1990 more than 26 million will live in North America.

One of the Hispanic pastors, Rev. Angel Perez, who shepherds a congregation in Cleveland, Ohio, became so involved in the lay ministry that he left his position as assistant manager of a supermarket and took a part-time job with half the pay. The Lord moved him to attend the LCMS Hispanic Institute in Chicago, which provides Spanish-speaking classes and professors. After two years of intensive study he was ordained.

With the high rate of mobility and the population increase, new church buildings must be built in the growing parts of our country. The *Laborers for Christ,* retired and semiretired construction workers and helpers, began building churches throughout the West in 1980. Millions of dollars were saved as a result of the volunteer labor.

The program became national and was endorsed

by the LCMS in 1983. In 1986 Laborers worked on 30 projects in 17 states. Several hundred persons have joined the group, which continues to grow.

... AND OTHERS

Many other kinds of mission outreach are carried out by the LCMS: college campus ministries, blind and deaf work, Armed Forces ministry, and the opening of new missions, especially in Florida, Texas, and California, three states with great population growth. The LCMS has set a goal to "plant" 500 new congregations every year.

OVERSEAS

In session 32 we noted that *Brazil* has been the most prosperous overseas mission effort of the LCMS. Now *Africa* appears to be the greatest challenge. Ten million Christians lived there in 1900; today they number over 200 million. By the year 2000 it is believed that there will be 400 million. Christianity will have grown from 9 percent to 48 percent within our century alone.

For example, LCMS Missionary Phil Sipes began work in Nakparikonkok, *Ghana,* hoping to teach the village leaders and others a few years before baptizing them.

"But some young men in the village already had faith and pressured the leaders to either accept or reject with good reason what I said," recounts Sipes. "They forced me to give God's answer to these sayings and teachings so that the elders could be convinced. They were successful, and I baptized 150 people in that village, including many elders. God has encouraged us by showing us some of the fruits of the work."

God has opened doors in *Korea,* as well. The first three LCMS missionaries began work there in 1958. A seminary was built near Seoul in 1983 and in three years graduated 75 native pastors. Since 1960 more than 670,000 persons have enrolled in the Bible correspondence program sponsored by the Lutheran Church of Korea.

LCMS mission work in *New Guinea* began in 1948, and now the Gutnius Lutheran Church has over 60,000 members among the 200,000 inhabitants of Enga Province, with 140 pastors and 300 teachers. Fifty students are enrolled at the Birip seminary. Carson Bjornstad, an LCMS teacher in the Gutnius Church, visited a village after learning that an enemy tribe had burned the classrooms and teachers' homes to the ground. People stayed away because of tension between the clans. He wrote:

"Olga, the education secretary for the Gutnius Church, spoke of the need to live in forgiveness and to put away grudges. He spoke of Christ's love and of His presence in their hearts. He prayed with them that God would grant them the strength to forgive their enemies and to proceed with the work. The Spirit of God was indeed with him and speaking through him. The people knew it, and their hearts went out to us as well. Pray with us that the people of this region may be reconciled to one another and be allowed to keep their school" (*A Report on Missions,* 1986).

SUPPORT

The LCMS supports and offers consultation to partner churches and mission fields in 38 countries representing every continent. Our 185 missionaries and all of the expenses connected with missions cost close to $10 million a year. In addition to sending contributions to the LCMS, 270 congregations "sponsor" 91 specific missionaries (totaling $2 million in five years).

What can we do to help? Give from the gifts God gives us, of course. But Jesus said, **"The harvest is plentiful but the workers are few. Ask the Lord of the harvest, therefore, to send out workers into His harvest field"** (Matthew 9:37–38).

FOR DISCUSSION

1. What two factors make mission outreach today so important?
2. What mission endeavors of the LCMS in the United States do you know about?
3. Why is it so important for the LCMS to carry out mission activities among people who do not have a European background? How can we do that effectively?
4. Laborers for Christ uses retired and semiretired workers. What are some other ways the church might use these people?
5. Why is it important to train natives of Korea, New Guinea, and other countries to carry out their own ministries?
6. If you were a missionary, what encouragement would you receive because a congregation "adopted you"?
7. What mission opportunities do you see for yourself? How can you take advantage of those opportunities?

A WORD FROM THE WORD

We give thanks to You, O God, we give thanks, for Your Name is near; men tell of Your wonderful deeds.

Psalm 75:1

SESSION 43

Training Professional Church Workers in The Lutheran Church— Missouri Synod

One generation will commend your works to another.

Psalm 145:4

Have you ever thought about becoming a full-time church worker, dedicating your life to God? You already know one or more persons—a pastor, teacher, deaconess, or some other individual—who has responded in this way to God's call.

Some congregations work hard at recruiting students for the 11 colleges and 4 seminaries of the LCMS. St. John Church, West Bend, WI, has supplied 40 full-time church workers in the last 20 years.

DO LUTHERAN SCHOOLS MAKE A DIFFERENCE?

In 1974 the results of a research study were published in Milo Brekke's *How Different Are People Who Attended Lutheran Schools?* (St. Louis: Concordia Publishing House). Those who attended Lutheran elementary and/or secondary schools
—report more frequent experiences with God in their personal lives;
—exhibit a more consistent belief in the divinity of Jesus;
—profess a greater clarity on the way of salvation by grace through faith in Jesus Christ alone (show more tendency to reject belief in salvation by works);
—display more Bible knowledge;
—engage in a much fuller devotional life;
—do more witnessing to others about Christ;
—hold a more balanced theology (not liberal, not ultraconservative), a balanced conservatism;
—have a greater awareness of the presence of the Trinity in their whole life;
—give a higher value to relationships with God and other persons;
—show more reasonable respect for authority;
—live out stronger tendencies to be forgiving and personally forthright with other people;
—evidence greater avoidance of oversimplistic views (e.g., views of social issues as mere power struggles);
—reveal less tendency to be anxious about their faith;
—are less swayed by their peers.

The research also indicated that the more years a person attended a Lutheran school, the more significant the difference became. These same qualities exist in many individuals who have not attended Lutheran schools, but it is less likely. The power to lead a Christian life is a free gift of the Holy Spirit working through the Word.

Another study of the effectiveness of Lutheran schools was reported by Ronald Johnstone in 1966 (Concordia Seminary, St. Louis) and 1983 (unpublished).

Johnstone included the influence of the family. He found that Lutheran school education was especially effective among students from families who were somewhat inactive in their churches, but made less of a difference among students from more active families. (Family influences account for more of the religious development in the latter group than in the former.)

Johnstone found that Lutheran schools were especially effective in teaching knowledge of the way to salvation. He also found significant differences in
—frequency of church attendance;
—financial contributions to church;
—belief in traditional doctrine of original sin;
—belief in the real presence in the Lord's Supper;
—belief in a young earth; and
—belief in the role of good works in salvation.

Johnstone found differences that were not significant or less significant in
—frequency of personal, private prayer;
—conduct of family devotions;
—belief in Biblical inspiration;
—belief in the existence of the devil; and
—belief in the universality of God's grace.

The differences in the latter three were not significant because all students scored high on them, regardless of whether or not they had attended a Lutheran school. Apparently these doctrines were taught well in Sunday school, confirmation instruction, and worship.

LORD, WHAT WOULD YOU HAVE ME DO?

Every year over 200 seminary graduates are needed to replace older *pastors* in the 6,200 congregations of the LCMS. If the opening of 100 new stations each year becomes a reality, even more men will be needed. Also, some serve in special ministries, such as military and hospital chaplaincies or ministries to the aged, minorities, or youth.

Qualifications for the pastoral office include a love for the Lord Jesus, sensitivity to people, a willingness to do serious study, a vigorous prayer life, and a cheerful and optimistic mood. Requirements for ordination include three years of study at an LCMS seminary after graduation from college and a year of internship (vicarage) before the final year. Graduates of synodical colleges begin their theological courses at those colleges.

Teachers are needed to staff the 1,600 Lutheran schools, including 70 high schools. Because of the demand, over one half of the vacancies in Lutheran schools in 1982 were filled by teachers who had not received synodical training. Teachers enjoy the great blessing God gives them when they take children, the lambs of Christ, on a daily walk with God and nourish them with His Word.

A *Director of Christian Education* (DCE) works with the pastor as a team, specializing in youth work, music, or evangelism, and assisting the pastor at divine services, teaching catechumens, or making calls. Most DCEs have Sunday school and vacation Bible school responsibilities. This calling requires four years of college plus a year of internship.

Deaconesses may carry out the functions of DCEs, or they may serve in church or state facilities for the aged and the mentally retarded. They also work as hospital chaplains, in prison ministries, and in social agencies.

Parish Assistants major in special areas of parish work, such as family life, education, and youth work. *Parish Workers* complete a five-semester college program in which they are prepared to serve primarily in church office management for congregations and agencies throughout the Synod.

A *Director of Evangelism* (DE) works with the pastor in evangelism activities. The DE must be
—qualified to enlist, motivate, train, and lead members of the parish in reaching out to the unchurched or the inactive;
—competent to teach in a variety of settings, such as Bible study groups, workshops, and seminars;
—adept at helping to cultivate a parish climate conducive to effective evangelism and successful assimilation of new members;
—trained for team ministry (able to work alongside professional parish staff and laity in planning and carrying out parish programs).

CHRISTIANS IN OTHER VOCATIONS

The 11 LCMS colleges do more than prepare full-time church workers. They also offer liberal arts programs and vocational training leading to many careers in the business world. Graduates include doctors, lawyers, musicians, bankers, and artists.

Why go to a Lutheran college rather than a secular university? A Concordia, Ann Arbor, graduate writes:

A liberal arts education provides the discipline and structure for perceiving the world around us. However, it does much more. It fosters Christian harmony and spiritual stamina to go out in that world and meet its challenges. My growth intellectually and spiritually made Concordia the single most positive influence in my life.

A nursing program, business administration, pre-law, computer and management information technology, accounting, finance—all learned in a Lutheran setting! A generation ago this was unheard of. We've read a lot of history; it's time to be a part of making it!

FOR DISCUSSION

1. As you see it, which of the "differences" in the Brekke and Johnstone reports are most obvious?
2. Discuss the role of the home in Christian education.
3. What qualifications, besides those listed, do you think a pastor should have?
4. Students usually have greater regard for certain teachers than for others. Why do you think highly of the "best" teacher you had in elementary school?
5. Which of the full-time church worker positions interest you the most? Why?
6. Why is a Lutheran college a good place to receive even a nonchurchworker education?

A WORD FROM THE WORD

Teach me, O Lord, to follow Your decrees; then I will keep them to the end. Give me understanding, and I will keep Your law and obey it with all my heart. Direct me in the path of Your commands, for there I find delight. Turn my heart toward Your statutes and not toward selfish gain.

Psalm 119:33–36

SESSION 44

Social Ministry in The Lutheran Church—Missouri Synod

He will deliver the needy who cry out, the afflicted who have no one to help. He will take pity on the weak and the needy and save the needy from death.
Ps. 72:12–13

—John, a 52-year-old farmer whose home, barns, and fields were auctioned so he could pay his debts still faces bankruptcy. What will happen next?

—June, a 17-year-old, four months pregnant, wonders how much longer she can hide it. What will her parents say? Should she have an abortion?

—Sengkham, a 37-year-old refugee from Laos, lives with his wife and children in a camp with hundreds of others. He waits for someone or something to help them begin a new life somewhere.

—George, a 60-year-old alcoholic, gets fired from yet another job. He worries and wonders.

What have they in common? Fear about the future.

NOT MY PROBLEM?

When asked, **"Who is my neighbor?" (Luke 10:29),** Jesus told the story of the Good Samaritan, adding, **"Go and do likewise" (verse 37).** He pressed the point in His narration of what will occur on Judgment Day: **"Whatever you did for one of the least of these . . . you did for Me" (Matthew 25:40).**

Jesus Himself stands behind the face of every person in need of our help. But too often our response demonstrates the axiom "Everybody's business is nobody's business." So thoughtful, compassionate, caring Christians have organized to meet the challenge that we call "social ministry."

SOCIAL MINISTRY?

Social ministry is the Love of God reaching out through His people, the Church, ministering compassionately to the entire spectrum of human need—the spiritual, physical, emotional, social and economic. It is loving care for people on the part of those who by faith have received the saving and enabling care of a loving God. The scope of social ministry is broad, encompassing all that Christians do to prevent and relieve human distress and to promote human development and well-being. Its focus, however, is narrow in that whatever is undertaken is based on the redemptive work of Jesus and endeavors to communicate Him to others as meaningfully as possible through the help that is extended. . . .

It is as important to distinguish social ministry from the Gospel as it is to relate it inseparably to the Gospel. The Gospel is always and only the message that God, in love, has reconciled fallen humanity to Himself through the incarnation, crucifixion and resurrection of His Son. Those who accept this love by faith necessarily respond with love for their fellow human beings. As Christians confront the diverse needs of other people, they are moved and guided by God's love towards that thoughtful and vigorous action which is social ministry. The Gospel is the cause, Social Ministry is the result.

Christians intent on meeting human need sometimes incorrectly equate social ministry and other efforts at human betterment with the Gospel. For example, the Social Gospel movement tended to identify progress toward a more humane and equitable society with the Gospel. Liberation Theology regards rescuing the victims of political and economic injustice as an essential element of the Gospel. In both cases the Gospel is being confused with things which may be, in part, a result of the Gospel (Social Ministry, Where Do We Go from Here: Blueprint for the Decade Ahead, *LCMS Board for Social Ministry Services, November 1985, pages 6–7).*

HOW DID IT START?

Late in 1838, 750 German Lutherans left their native Saxony and settled in Perry County and St. Louis, MO. Among them (although he traveled via New York rather than New Orleans) was a stocky, practical-minded man, age 30, named Johann Buenger. He suffered one tragedy after another during the next 20 years. His wife and three little sons died, and two of his four daughters from a second wife died before reaching adulthood.

Rather than becoming bitter and distraught, Pastor Buenger took affirmative action to fight the disease that took his loved ones from him. Largely through his efforts, rooms in homes (and later, entire buildings) were used as hospitals. An asylum for the aged and an orphanage were also built. In the years that followed, hospitals, orphanages, and homes for the elderly were established by Lutherans in many places throughout the country.

CAN WE WORK TOGETHER?

Lutheran of other synods also became active in social ministry. Pooling their efforts seemed to be the most effective way of caring for the lonely, sick, and addicted. Today we find in America 55 pan-Lutheran agencies and 25 agencies operated solely by congregations of the Missouri Synod.

FACELESS STATISTICS?

In our world 25,000 persons die every day due to starvation or hunger-related problems. Fifteen thousand of these are children; the number of deaths resulting from the bombing of Hiroshima equals three days of deaths from malnutrition.

In America the number affected by alcoholism and drug addiction continues to grow. According to conservative figures, 13 of every 300 members over age 21 in an average Lutheran congregation have a severe drinking problem. A third of all 7th-graders in our country use marijuana. One half of suburban high school students try cocaine, and 10 percent are regular users. Each year 4,000 persons between the ages of 16 and 19 are killed in alcohol-related accidents.

Chemical dependence (alcoholism, drug addiction) is an illness of body, mind, and spirit. Unlike other illnesses, it cannot be conquered with medication or surgery, but through self-awareness, insight, and willingness to seek help.

Teenage pregnancy is another source of concern in our society. A person with a "crisis" pregnancy needs a caring friend to counsel her about the helpful services available during and after her pregnancy. Without this help, she may be pressured into assuming that an abortion is a safe, easy solution, unaware of the possible physical, mental, emotional, and spiritual risks abortion brings. Because of fear of judgment, she may hesitate to inform those closest to her of her pregnancy.

Two other person-problems abound at this time: refugees from overseas who have no place to live, and Midwestern farmers who are losing their property and possessions.

WHAT IS THE CHURCH DOING ABOUT THIS?

The Missouri Synod joins hearts and hands with other Lutherans in Lutheran World Relief efforts. Millions of dollars annually are collected and spent on food, clothing, and medicines to alleviate the suffering. As a result, millions of lives were saved in the Darfur area of northwest Sudan, Africa, alone, during the past few years.

Extensive resources are being provided for those suffering from chemical dependency. National organizations such as Alcoholics Anonymous and Al-Anon groups have been a blessing to many. These people "gain control," though the illness lasts a lifetime. Similarly, Crisis Pregnancy Centers and Lutheran Social Ministries are equipped to help girls and women in need of compassion and guidance.

Since 1975 congregations of the Missouri Synod have sponsored 70,000 refugees who fled from Asia and Europe to escape persecution in their native lands.

During the past decade a number of farmers who lost their barns, fields, equipment, homes, and lands have been helped through agricommunity seminars and Bible studies. Often the solution results in a career change, but the individual still needs to deal with emotions, such as anger toward God and bankers, loss of self-respect, and feelings of futility.

FOR DISCUSSION

1. Which teachings of Jesus call us to be compassionate and to help those in need? What motivates Christians to follow Jesus' commands?
2. What is social ministry?
3. How does social ministry differ from the Social Gospel and liberation theology?
4. Describe your congregation's plan for social ministry. Do you think it carries out its plan effectively? Explain. How can you help?
5. How would you help a friend who is chemically dependent or pregnant?

A WORD FROM THE WORD

Do not let the oppressed retreat in disgrace; may the poor and needy praise Your name.
Psalm 74:21

SESSION 45

Concluding Activities for Unit 5

TERMS

Write brief descriptions of the terms that follow:
1. Theological embellishment
2. Fact Finding Committee
3. Seminex
4. Hispanics
5. North American Missions
6. Laborers for Christ
7. Brekke report
8. Social ministry
9. Liberation theology
10. Chemical dependence
11. Refugees
12. Agricommunity crisis

SHORT ANSWERS

Write a short answer to each of the following questions.
1. What attitude toward Scripture did the 1973 convention of the Missouri Synod condemn?
2. Why did the president of the Synod initiate a fact-finding investigation at Concordia Seminary, St. Louis?
3. When and why did members of the faculty and student body "walk out" and form Seminex?
4. Which two factors make mission outreach particularly important today?
5. How does the Korean church reach out to people?
6. Which continent is rapidly becoming Christianized?
7. Which findings of the Brekke and Johnstone reports seem especially significant?
8. What special qualifications should a person have if he wants to be a pastor?
9. How do deaconesses serve the church?
10. Why is it advantageous even for a person not going into full-time church work to attend a Lutheran college?
11. Why do Christians carry out social ministry?
12. In what way does Lutheran World Relief help people?